JOHN
MACARTHUR

D1054262

1, 2, 3 JOHN
JUDE

Established in Truth, Marked by Love

THOMAS NELSON
Since 1798

NASHVILLE   DALLAS   MEXICO CITY   RIO DE JANEIRO

CONTENTS

Introduction to 1 John

The epistle's title has always been "1 John." It is the first and largest in a series of three epistles that bear the apostle John's name. Since the letter identifies no specific church, location, or individual to whom it was sent, its classification is as a "general epistle." Although 1 John does not exhibit some of the general characteristics of an epistle common to that time (e.g., no introduction, greeting, or concluding salutation), its intimate tone and content indicate that the term *epistle* still applies to it.

AUTHOR AND DATE

The epistle does not identify the author, but the strong, consistent and earliest testimony of the church ascribes it to John, the disciple and apostle (see Luke 6:13–14). This anonymity strongly affirms the early church's identification of the epistle with John the apostle, for only someone of John's well-known and preeminent status as an apostle would be able to write with such unmistakable authority, expecting complete obedience from his readers, without clearly identifying himself (e.g., 4:6). He was well-known to the readers, so he didn't need to mention his name.

John and James, his older brother (Acts 12:2), were known as "the sons of Zebedee" (Matt. 10:2–4), to whom Jesus gave the name "Sons of Thunder" (Mark 3:17). John was one of the three most intimate associates of Jesus (along with Peter and James—see Matt. 17:1; 26:37), being an eyewitness to and participant in Jesus' earthly ministry (1:1–4). In addition to the three epistles, John also authored the fourth Gospel, in which he identified himself as the disciple "whom Jesus loved" and as the one who reclined on Jesus' breast at the Last Supper (John 13:23; 19:26; 20:2; 21:7, 20). He also wrote the book of Revelation (Rev. 1:1).

Precise dating is difficult because no clear historical indications of date exist in 1 John. Most likely John composed this work in the latter part of the first century. Church tradition consistently identifies John in his advanced age as living and actively writing during this time at Ephesus in Asia Minor. The tone of the epistle supports this evidence since the writer gives the strong impression that he is much older than his readers (e.g., "my little children"—2:1, 18, 28). The epistle and John's gospel reflect similar vocabulary and manner of expression. Such similarity causes many to date the writing of John's epistles as occurring soon after he composed his gospel. Since many date the gospel of

1

John during the later part of the first century, they also prefer a similar date for the epistles. Furthermore, the heresy John combats most likely reflects the beginnings of Gnosticism, which was in its early stages during the latter third of the first century, when John was actively writing. Since no mention is made of the persecution under Domitian, which began about AD 95, it may have been written before that began. In light of such factors, a reasonable date for 1 John is ca. AD 90–95. It was likely written from Ephesus to the churches of Asia Minor over which John exercised apostolic leadership.

BACKGROUND AND SETTING

Although he was greatly advanced in age when he penned this epistle, John was still actively ministering to churches. He was the sole remaining apostolic survivor who had intimate, eyewitness association with Jesus throughout His earthly ministry, death, resurrection, and ascension. The church Fathers (e.g., Justin Martyr, Irenaeus, Clement of Alexandria, Eusebius) indicate that after that time, John lived at Ephesus in Asia Minor, carrying out an extensive evangelistic program, overseeing many of the churches that had arisen, and conducting an extensive writing ministry (e.g., epistles, the gospel of John, and Revelation). One church Father (Papias), who had direct contact with John, described him as a "living and abiding voice." As the last remaining apostle, John's testimony was highly authoritative among the churches. Many eagerly sought to hear the one who had firsthand experience with the Lord Jesus.

Ephesus (see Acts 19:10) lay within the intellectual center of Asia Minor. As predicted years before by the apostle Paul (Acts 20:28–31), false teachers arising from within the church's own ranks, saturated with the prevailing climate of philosophical trends, began infecting the church with false doctrine, perverting fundamental apostolic teaching. These false teachers advocated new ideas, which eventually became known as "Gnosticism" (from the Greek word "knowledge"). After the Pauline battle for freedom from the law, Gnosticism was the most dangerous heresy that threatened the early church during the first three centuries. Most likely, John was combating the beginnings of this virulent heresy that threatened to destroy the fundamentals of the faith and the churches.

Gnosticism, influenced by such philosophers as Plato, advocated a dualism and asserted that matter was inherently evil, and spirit was good. As a result of this presupposition, these false teachers, although attributing some form of deity to Christ, denied His true humanity to preserve Him from evil. It also claimed elevated knowledge, a higher truth known only to those in on the deep things. Only the initiated had the mystical knowledge of truth that was higher even than the Scriptures.

2

Instead of divine revelation standing as judge over man's ideas, man's ideas judged God's revelation (2:15–17). The heresy featured two basic forms. First, some asserted that Jesus' physical body was not real but only "seemed" to be physical (known as "Docetism," from a Greek word that means "to appear"). John forcefully affirmed the physical reality of Jesus by reminding his readers that he was an eyewitness to Him ("heard," "seen," " handled," "Jesus Christ has come in the flesh"—1:1–4; 4:2–3). According to early tradition (Irenaeus), another form of this heresy which John may have attacked was led by a man named Cerinthus, who contended that the Christ's "spirit" descended on the human Jesus at His baptism but left Him just before His crucifixion. John wrote that the Jesus who was baptized at the beginning of His ministry was the same person who was crucified on the cross (5:6).

Such heretical views destroy not only the true humanity of Jesus, but also the atonement, for Jesus must not only have been truly God but also the truly human (and physically real) man who actually suffered and died on the cross in order to be the acceptable substitutionary sacrifice for sin (see Heb. 2:14–17). The biblical view of Jesus affirms His complete humanity as well as His full deity.

The Gnostic idea that matter is evil and only spirit is good led to the idea that either the body should be treated harshly—a form of asceticism (e.g., Col. 2:21–23)—or sin committed in the body had no connection or effect on one's spirit. This led some, especially John's opponents, to conclude that sin committed in the physical body did not matter; absolute indulgence in immorality was permissible; one could deny sin even existed (1:8–10) and disregard God's law (3:4). John emphasized the need for obedience to God's laws, for he defined the true love of God as obedience to His commandments (5:3).

A lack of love for fellow believers characterizes false teachers, especially as they react against anyone rejecting their new way of thinking (3:10–18). They separated their deceived followers from the fellowship of those who remained faithful to apostolic teaching, leading John to reply that such separation outwardly manifested that those who followed false teachers lacked genuine salvation (2:19). Their departure left the other believers, who remained faithful to apostolic doctrine, shaken. Responding to this crisis, the aged apostle wrote to reassure those remaining faithful and to combat this grave threat to the church. Since the heresy was so acutely dangerous and the time period was so critical for the church in danger of being overwhelmed by false teaching, John gently, lovingly, but with unquestionable apostolic authority, sent this letter to churches in his sphere of influence to stem this spreading plague of false doctrine.

HISTORICAL AND THEOLOGICAL THEMES

In light of the circumstances of the epistle, the overall theme of 1 John is "a recall to the fundamentals of the faith" or "back to the basics of Christianity." The apostle deals with certainties, not opinions or conjecture. He expresses the absolute character of Christianity in very simple terms; terms that are clear and unmistakable, leaving no doubt as to the fundamental nature of those truths. He uses a warm, conversational, and, above all, loving tone, like a father having a tender, intimate conversation with his children.

First John also is pastoral, written from the heart of a pastor who has concern for his people. As a shepherd, John communicated to his flock some very basic, but vital principles that reassured them regarding the basics of their faith. He desired them to be joyful in the certainty of their faith, rather than be upset by the false teaching and current defections of some (1:4).

The book's viewpoint, however, is not only pastoral but also polemical, not only positive but also negative. John refutes the defectors, exhibiting no tolerance for those who pervert divine truth. He labels those departing from the truth as "false prophets" (4:1), "those who try to deceive" (2:26; 3:7), and "antichrists" (2:18). He pointedly identifies the ultimate source of all such defection from sound doctrine as demonic (4:1–7).

The constant repetition of three subthemes reinforces the overall theme regarding faithfulness to the basics of Christianity: happiness (1:4), holiness (2:1), and security (5:13). By faithfulness to the basics, his readers will experience these three results continually in their lives. These three factors also reveal the key cycle of true spirituality in 1 John: a proper belief in Jesus produces obedience to His commands; obedience produces love for God and fellow believers (e.g., 3:23–24). When these three (sound faith, obedience, love) operate in concert together, they result in happiness, holiness, and assurance. They constitute the evidence, the litmus test, of a true Christian.

INTERPRETIVE CHALLENGES

Theologians debate the precise nature of the false teachers' beliefs in 1 John, because John does not directly specify their beliefs, but rather combats the heretics mainly through a positive restatement of the fundamentals of the faith. The main feature of the heresy, as noted above, seems to be a denial of the Incarnation, i.e., Christ had not come in the flesh. This was most likely an incipient or beginning form of Gnosticism, as noted previously.

The interpreter is also challenged by the rigidity of John's theology. John presents the basics or fundamentals of the Christian life in absolute, not relative, terms. Unlike Paul, who presented exceptions, and dealt so often with believers' failures to meet the divine standard, John does not deal with the "what if I fail?" issues. Only in 2:1–2 does he give some relief from the absolutes. The rest of the book presents truths in black and white rather than shades of gray, often through a stark contrast, e.g., "light" vs. "darkness" (1:5, 7; 2:8–11); truth vs. lies (2:21–22; 4:1); children of God vs. children of the devil (3:10). Those who claim to be Christians must absolutely display the characteristics of genuine Christians: sound doctrine, obedience, and love. Those who are truly born-again have been given a new nature, which gives evidence of itself. Those who do not display characteristics of the new nature don't have it, so were never truly born again. The issues do not center (as much of Paul's writing does) in maintaining temporal or daily fellowship with God but the application of basic tests in one's life to confirm that salvation has truly occurred. Such absolute distinctions are also characteristic of John's gospel.

In a unique fashion, John challenges the interpreter by his repetition of similar themes over and over which emphasize the basic truths about genuine Christianity. Some have likened John's repetition to a spiral that moves outward, becoming larger and larger, each time spreading the same truth over a wider area and encompassing more territory. Others have seen the spiral as moving inward, penetrating deeper and deeper into the same themes while expanding on his thoughts. However one views the spiraling pattern, John uses repetition of basic truths as a means to accentuate their importance and to help his readers understand and remember them.

Notes

CHRIST AND SIN

DRAWING NEAR

The apostle John was older when he wrote these three little epistles. His mature faith and godly example come through strongly. It is always a blessing to spend time with an older saint—someone who has known the Lord and walked with Him for a long time. List one or two "mentors" in your life, those mature Christians you greatly respect. Describe some of their unique qualities.

_____

_____

_____

_____

_____

THE CONTEXT

As an eyewitness to Jesus' ministry, including His death and resurrection, and as one of the three most intimate associates of the Lord (together with Peter and James), John begins his first epistle by affirming the physical reality of Jesus Christ's having come "in the flesh" (see 4:2–3 NKJV). In this way, John accentuated the gravity of the false teaching that was permeating the church. He strongly affirmed the historical reality of Jesus' humanity and the certainty of the gospel. Although the false teachers of John's day claimed to believe in Christ, their denial of the true nature of Christ (i.e., His humanity) demonstrated their lack of genuine salvation. This affirmation of a proper view of Christ constitutes the first test of genuine fellowship.

Next, John affirms the reality of sin, in order to counter the false teachers who denied the existence or importance of sin. This was a second test of fellowship: Those who deny the reality of sin demonstrate their lack of genuine salvation.

KEYS TO THE TEXT

Confess: This word comes from the Greek word *homologeo,* and means "to say the same thing." To confess our sins means to agree with God about them. This is a characteristic of all true Christians. They agree with God about their sin. That means they hate their sin; they don't love it. They acknowledge that they are sinful, and yet they know they are forgiven and that they have an Advocate with the Father.

Advocate: The Greek word is *parakletos*, literally, "one who is called to our side." This Greek term refers to the position of a comforter, consoler, or defense attorney. John 16:7 translates this word as "Helper" (literally "one called alongside"). Perhaps a modern concept of the term would be a defense attorney. Although Satan prosecutes believers night and day before the Father regarding their sin, Christ's High-Priestly ministry guarantees acquittal. In John 14:26 and 15:26, the Holy Spirit is called the Advocate for believers. The Holy Spirit works within us to comfort and help us and also pleads our case before the Father in heaven.

Unleashing the Text

Read 1 John 1:1–2:2, noting the key words and definitions next to the passage.

1 John 1:1–2:2 (NKJV)

That which (v. 1)—refers to the proclamation of the gospel that centers in Christ's Person, words, and works as contained in apostolic testimony

from the beginning (v. 1)— When the readers first heard about Jesus (see 2:7, 24). The phrase emphasizes the stability of the gospel message. Its contents do not change but remain stable from the very beginning. It is not subject to change due to current worldly fads or philosophical thinking.

1 *That which was from the beginning, which we have heard, which we have seen with our eyes, which we have looked upon, and our hands have handled, concerning the Word of life—*

2 *the life was manifested, and we have seen, and bear witness, and declare to you that eternal life which was with the Father and was manifested to us—*

3 *that which we have seen and heard we declare to you, that you also may have fellowship with us; and truly our fellowship is with the Father and with His Son Jesus Christ.*

we have heard . . . we have seen . . . we have looked upon . . . our hands have handled (v. 1)—The words used here point to the physical reality of Jesus, for a spirit cannot be heard, gazed at for long periods ("looked upon"), or touched ("handled") as Jesus was by John during His earthly ministry and even after His resurrection.

manifested . . . seen . . . bear witness . . . heard . . . declare (vv. 2–3)—John dramatically reemphasizes the authority of his own personal experience as an eyewitness of Jesus' life, in contrast with the false teachers who had never seen or known Christ.

fellowship with us (v. 3)—Fellowship does not mean social relations, but that his readers were to be partakers (partners) with John in possessing eternal life. Here it is equated with salvation.

4 And these things we write to you that your joy may be full.

5 This is the message which we have heard from Him and declare to you, that God is light and in Him is no darkness at all.

6 If we say that we have fellowship with Him, and walk in darkness, we lie and do not practice the truth.

7 But if we walk in the light as He is in the light, we have fellowship with one another, and the blood of Jesus Christ His Son cleanses us from all sin.

8 If we say that we have no sin, we deceive ourselves, and the truth is not in us.

9 If we confess our sins, He is faithful and just to forgive us our sins and to cleanse us from all unrighteousness.

10 If we say that we have not sinned, we make Him a liar, and His word is not in us.

2:1 My little children, these things I write to you, so that you may not sin. And if anyone sins, we have an Advocate with the Father, Jesus Christ the righteous.

2 And He Himself is the propitiation for our sins, and not for ours only but also for the whole world.

your joy may be full (v. 4)—A main goal for this epistle is to create joy in the readers. The proclamation of the reality of the gospel (vv. 1–2) produces a fellowship in eternal life (v. 3), and in turn, fellowship in eternal life produces joy (v. 4).

we have heard from Him (v. 5)—The message that John and the other apostles preached came from God, not from men (see Gal. 1:12).

God is light (v. 5)—In Scripture, "light" refers to biblical truth or holiness and purity, while "darkness" refers to error or falsehood, sin or wrongdoing.

no darkness at all (v. 5)—With this phrase, John forcefully affirms that God is absolutely perfect and nothing exists in His character that impinges on His truth and holiness (see James 1:17).

do not practice (v. 6)—This points to their habitual failure regarding the practice of the truth.

make Him a liar (v. 10)—Since God has said that all people are sinners (see Ps. 14:3; 51:5; Isa. 53:6; Jer. 17:5–6; Rom. 3:10–19, 23; 6:23), to deny that fact is to blaspheme God with slander that defames His name.

so that you may not sin (2:1)—Although a Christian must continually acknowledge and confess sin (1:9), he is not powerless against it. Fulfilling the duty of confession does not give license to sin. Sin can and should be conquered through the power of the Holy Spirit.

for the whole world (v. 2)—This is a generic term, referring not to every single individual, but to mankind in general; Christ actually paid the penalty only for those who would repent and believe.

1) In verses 1–4, John stated his purpose for writing this epistle. What was that purpose?

_____

_____

_____

_____

2) How did John describe his experience with Christ in the opening sentences of his epistle?

_____

_____

_____

_____

_____

3) What does the Bible mean when it says God is light? (Use a concordance to look up other verses that refer to God in these terms.)

_____

_____

_____

_____

4) What did John mean by the phrase "walk in the light"? What does this manner of life demonstrate?

_____

_____

_____

_____

5) According to John, what are the signs that a person is deceived and not living by the truth?

_____

_____

_____

_____

_____

6) What is God's response to those who honestly confess their sins?

_____

_____

_____

_____

_____

GOING DEEPER

For more insight about light and darkness, read Romans 13:11–14.

11 *And do this, knowing the time, that now it is high time to awake out of sleep; for now our salvation is nearer than when we first believed.*

12 *The night is far spent, the day is at hand. Therefore let us cast off the works of darkness, and let us put on the armor of light.*

13 *Let us walk properly, as in the day, not in revelry and drunkenness, not in lewdness and lust, not in strife and envy.*

14 *But put on the Lord Jesus Christ, and make no provision for the flesh, to fulfill its lusts.*

EXPLORING THE MEANING

7) What added insights does the apostle Paul provide in Romans 13 about the importance of being light in the midst of a dark world? How does he contrast these two ways of living?

_____

_____

_____

_____

8) Why was John so adamant in the opening paragraph of his epistle about his firsthand experience with Christ?

_____

_____

_____

_____

9) What does confession have to do with gaining forgiveness in 1 John 1:9? How is admission of sin and guilt a prerequisite to salvation?

_____

_____

_____

_____

10) Why did John have such a high view of Christ, the "Word of life"?

_____

_____

_____

_____

TRUTH FOR TODAY

Many people doubt whether Jesus ever really existed, but many historians have written about the Lord Jesus Christ. Around AD 114, the Roman historian Tacitus wrote that the founder of the Christian religion, Jesus Christ, was put to death by Pontius Pilate in the reign of the Roman emperor Tiberius (*Annals* 15.44). In AD 90, the Jewish historian Josephus penned a short biographical note on Jesus: "Now there was about this time Jesus, a wise man, if it be lawful to call Him a man, for He was a doer of wonderful works, a teacher of such men as received the truth with pleasure. He drew over to Him both many of the Jews and many of the Gentiles. He was Christ" (*Antiquities* 18.63). Jesus was a man in history. And His claims are true.

REFLECTING ON THE TEXT

11) John began this epistle by telling of his personal encounter with Jesus. What is *your* testimony to the reality of Christ? When did you first know He is the way, the truth, and the life, and when did you put your faith in Him?

_____

_____

_____

_____

12) Are you walking in the light and living in joy because of your fellowship with Christ and other believers? If not, what sins do you need to confess and forsake today?

_____

_____

_____

_____

_____

Personal Response

Write out additional reflections, questions you may have, or a prayer.

_____

_____

_____

_____

_____

_____

_____

_____

_____

_____

_____

_____

_____

_____

_____

_____

ADDITIONAL NOTES

Obedience and Love

Drawing Near

If a stranger approached you on the street corner and asked, "What must I do to be saved?" how would you respond?

_____

_____

_____

_____

_____

If that same stranger inquired, "Tell me how you know *for sure* that you are right with God and headed for heaven," how would you respond?

_____

_____

_____

_____

The Context

The first chapter of 1 John presents a doctrinal test of genuine salvation. Here in chapter 2, John cites a moral test of genuine fellowship: obedience to God's commands. While subjective assurance of salvation comes through the internal witness of the Holy Spirit (see 1 John 5:10), the test of obedience constitutes objective assurance that one is genuinely saved. John's argument is that obedience is the external, visible proof of salvation. The false teachers' failure to obey God's commands objectively demonstrated that they were not saved. Those who are truly enlightened and know God will be obedient to His Word.

Another aspect of the moral test of genuine fellowship is *love*. The primary focus of the moral test is obedience to the command of love, because love is the fulfillment of the law and is also Christ's new command (Matt. 22:34–40; John 15:12, 17). True enlightenment is to love. God's light is the light of love, so to walk in light is to walk in love.

KEYS TO THE TEXT

World: This term comes from the Greek word *kosmos*. It does not refer to the physical earth or universe, but rather to the spiritual reality of the man-centered, Satan-directed system of this present age. It refers to the self-centered, godless value system and mores of fallen mankind. The goal of the world is self-glory, self-fulfillment, self-indulgence, self-satisfaction, and every other form of self-service, all of which amount to hostility toward God.

UNLEASHING THE TEXT

Read 1 John 2:3–17, noting the key words and definitions next to the passage.

1 John 2:3–17 (NKJV)

know . . . keep (vv. 3–4)—The repetition of these words emphasizes that those who are genuinely born again display the habit of obedience. That these two words are among John's favorites is clear since he uses "know" approximately forty times and "keep" approximately ten times in this epistle.

abides (v. 6)—one of John's favorite terms for salvation

just as He walked (v. 6)—Jesus' life of obedience is the Christian's pattern.

new (v. 7)—Not "new" in the sense of time but something that is fresh in quality, kind, or form; something that replaces something else that has been worn out. The commandment of love was "new" because Jesus personified love in a fresh, new way, and it was manifested in believers' hearts (Rom. 5:5) and energized by the Holy Spirit (Gal. 5:22; 1 Thess. 4:9).

from the beginning (v. 7)—This phrase refers not to the beginning of time but the beginning of their Christian lives, from the day of their salvation.

hates (v. 9)—The original language conveys the idea of someone who habitually hates or is marked by a lifestyle of hate.

3 Now by this we know that we know Him, if we keep His commandments.

4 He who says, "I know Him," and does not keep His commandments, is a liar, and the truth is not in him.

5 But whoever keeps His word, truly the love of God is perfected in him. By this we know that we are in Him.

6 He who says he abides in Him ought himself also to walk just as He walked.

7 Brethren, I write no new commandment to you, but an old commandment which you have had from the beginning. The old commandment is the word which you heard from the beginning.

8 Again, a new commandment I write to you, which thing is true in Him and in you, because the darkness is passing away, and the true light is already shining.

9 He who says he is in the light, and hates his brother, is in darkness until now.

10 He who loves his brother abides in the light, and there is no cause for stumbling in him.

11 But he who hates his brother is in darkness and walks in darkness, and does not know where he is going, because the darkness has blinded his eyes.

12 *I write to you, little children, because your sins are forgiven you for His name's sake.*

13 *I write to you, fathers, because you have known Him who is from the beginning. I write to you, young men, because you have overcome the wicked one. I write to you, little children, because you have known the Father.*

14 *I have written to you, fathers, because you have known Him who is from the beginning. I have written to you, young men, because you are strong, and the word of God abides in you, and you have overcome the wicked one.*

15 *Do not love the world or the things in the world. If anyone loves the world, the love of the Father is not in him.*

16 *For all that is in the world—the lust of the flesh, the lust of the eyes, and the pride of life—is not of the Father but is of the world.*

17 *And the world is passing away, and the lust of it; but he who does the will of God abides forever.*

I write . . . I have written (vv. 12, 14)—"I write" is from John's perspective, while "I have written" anticipates his readers' perspective when they received the letter.

fathers . . . young men . . . little children (vv. 13–14)—These very clear distinctions identify three stages of spiritual growth in God's family: "Fathers," the most mature, have a deep knowledge of the eternal God; "young men" are those who, while not yet having the mature experience of knowing God in the Word and through life, do know sound doctrine; "little children" are those who have only the basic awareness of God and need to grow.

Do not love the world (v. 15)—Although John often repeats the importance of love and that God is love (4:7–8), he also reveals that God hates a certain type of love: love of the world (John 15:18–20).

the love of the Father is not in him (v. 15)—One is either a genuine Christian, marked by love and obedience to God, or one is a non-Christian in rebellion against God, i.e., in love with and enslaved by the world (Eph. 2:1–3; Col. 1:13; James 4:4). No middle ground between these two alternatives exists for someone claiming to be born-again.

all that is in the world (v. 16)—While the world's philosophies and ideologies and much that it offers may appear attractive and appealing, that is deception—its true and pervasive nature is evil, harmful, ruinous, and satanic. Its deadly theories are raised up against the knowledge of God and hold the souls of men captive (2 Cor. 10:3–5).

lust (v. 16)—John uses the term negatively here for a strong desire for evil things.

flesh (v. 16)—The term refers to the sin nature of man—the rebellious self, dominated by sin and in opposition to God—which Satan incites using the things of this world.

eyes (v. 16)—Satan uses the eyes as a strategic avenue to incite wrong desires (Josh. 7:20–21; 2 Sam. 11:2; Matt. 5:27–29).

the pride of life (v. 16)—The phrase has the idea of arrogance over one's circumstances, which produces haughtiness or exaggeration and involves parading one's possessions to impress other people (James 4:16).

the world is passing away (v. 17)—The Christian also must not love the satanic world system because of its temporary nature. It is in the continual process of disintegration, headed for destruction (Rom. 8:18–22).

he who does the will of God abides forever (v. 17)—In contrast to the temporary world, God's will is permanent and unchangeable, and those who follow God's will abide as His people forever.

1) What is obedience, and why is it essential in the Christian life?

_____

_____

_____

_____

_____

2) What did John mean when he said that we must walk as Jesus did?

_____

_____

_____

_____

_____

3) In verses 9 and 10, John presented another test of true fellowship. What is it?

_____

_____

_____

_____

_____

4) To what three groups of people was John writing? What do these descriptive titles mean?

_____

_____

_____

_____

_____

5) What was John's strong warning in verses 15–17? What are the consequences of heeding/dismissing this command?

_____

_____

_____

_____

6) According to this passage, what are we supposed to love, and what are we *not* supposed to love?

_____

_____

_____

_____

_____

GOING DEEPER

The first man and woman were given a choice between loving the world and obeying God. For more insight, read Genesis 3:1–7.

1 *Now the serpent was more cunning than any beast of the field which the Lord God had made. And he said to the woman, "Has God indeed said, 'You shall not eat of every tree of the garden'?"*

2 *And the woman said to the serpent, "We may eat the fruit of the trees of the garden;*

3 *but of the fruit of the tree which is in the midst of the garden, God has said, 'You shall not eat it, nor shall you touch it, lest you die.'"*

4 *Then the serpent said to the woman, "You will not surely die.*

5 *For God knows that in the day you eat of it your eyes will be opened, and you will be like God, knowing good and evil."*

6 *So when the woman saw that the tree was good for food, that it was pleasant to the eyes, and a tree desirable to make one wise, she took of its fruit and ate. She also gave to her husband with her, and he ate.*

7 *Then the eyes of both of them were opened, and they knew that they were naked; and they sewed fig leaves together and made themselves coverings.*

EXPLORING THE MEANING

7) How does this Genesis account of the first temptation in Eden compare with and underscore the truth of John's words in 2:15–17?

_____

_____

_____

_____

8) We are to walk as Jesus walked (2:6). How specifically is Christ our example in the areas of obedience and love (that is, in loving people, but not loving the world system)?

_____

_____

_____

_____

9) Based on John's descriptions, what is the difference between "little children," "young men," and "fathers" (2:12–14)?

_____

_____

_____

_____

10) How can we tell if we are too enamored with the world?

_____

_____

_____

_____

TRUTH FOR TODAY

John's zeal for the truth shaped the way he wrote. Of all the writers of the New Testament, he is the most black-and-white in his thinking. He thinks and writes in absolutes. He deals with certainties. Everything is cut-and-dried with him. There aren't many gray areas in his teaching, because he tends to state things in unqualified, antithetical language. He tells us we are either walking in the light or dwelling in darkness. If we are born of God, we do not sin—indeed, we *cannot* sin. We are either "of God" or "of the world" (1 John 4:4–5 NKJV). If we love, we are born of God; and if we don't love, we are not born of God. John writes, "Whoever abides in Him does not sin. Whoever sins has neither seen Him nor known Him" (1 John 3:6 NKJV). He says all these things without qualification and without any softening of the hard lines.

REFLECTING ON THE TEXT

11) How do you respond to John's stark, black-and-white teaching about love, light, and the world (2:4, 9, 15)? Is it helpful? Why?

_____

_____

_____

_____

_____

12) The great Reformer Martin Luther once commented on the power of Scripture by declaring: "The Bible is alive, it speaks to me; it has feet, it runs after me; it has hands, it lays hold of me." What in this study is running after you and laying hold of your heart? What do you need to *do* with what you've learned here?

_____

_____

_____

_____

_____

Personal Response

Write out additional reflections, questions you may have, or a prayer.

3
ANTICHRISTS

1 John 2:18–27

DRAWING NEAR

John urges his readers to know the truth and watch out for counterfeits. Have you ever been scammed or deceived? What happened? How did you feel afterwards?

_____

_____

_____

_____

_____

Have you ever realized that one of your spiritual beliefs was erroneous? What happened to make you realize you were wrong?

_____

_____

_____

_____

THE CONTEXT

The aged apostle John warned his flock about the fundamental tests of genuine Christian fellowship. True believers, he insists, will pass the doctrinal test—they will subscribe to orthodox views of Christ and of sin. They will also pass the moral test—obeying the commands of Christ and loving the brethren (while *not* loving the world).

Now, in his unique literary style, John "spirals" back around through these same essential truths. By constantly repeating these themes (he does so four times) and examining them from various angles, he drives home these truths in the minds and hearts of his readers. In this section he speaks of false teachers (called "antichrists") who depart from the true Christian fellowship, deny the Christian faith, and deceive the Christian faithful. This serves to underscore the need for the people of God to make sure they are doctrinally astute and pure.

KEYS TO THE TEXT

Antichrist: This term is found only in John's epistles (1 John 2:18, 22; 4:3; 2 John 7). From the Greek word *antichristos* ("against/instead of Christ"), it refers to an enemy of Christ or one who seeks to usurp His rightful place. In 1 John 2:18 it is a proper name and refers to the coming, final world ruler, energized by Satan, who will seek to replace and oppose the true Christ. Its second usage (2:18) is plural and refers to the false teachers who were troubling John's congregations, because their false doctrine distorted the truth and opposed Christ. The term, therefore, refers to a principle of evil, incarnated in men, who are hostile and opposed to God.

UNLEASHING THE TEXT

Read 1 John 2:18–27, noting the key words and definitions next to the passage.

1 John 2:18–27 (NKJV)

the last hour (v. 18)—The phrase refers to the "latter times" or "last days," i.e., the time period between the first and second comings of Christ (1 Tim. 4:1; James 5:3; 1 Pet. 4:7; 2 Pet. 3:3; Jude 18).

18 *Little children, it is the last hour; and as you have heard that the Antichrist is coming, even now many antichrists have come, by which we know that it is the last hour.*

They went out from us . . . none of them were of us (v. 19)—The first characteristic mentioned of antichrists, i.e., false teachers and deceivers (vv. 22–26), is that they depart from the faithful; i.e., they arise from within the church and depart from true fellowship, leading people out with them.

19 *They went out from us, but they were not of us; for if they had been of us, they would have continued with us; but they went out that they might be made manifest, that none of them were of us.*

an anointing from the Holy One (v. 20)—The Holy Spirit guards believers from error (see Acts 10:38; 2 Cor. 1:21).

20 *But you have an anointing from the Holy One, and you know all things.*

21 *I have not written to you because you do not know the truth, but because you know it, and that no lie is of the truth.*

denies the Father and the Son (vv. 22–23)—A second characteristic of antichrists is that they deny the faith (i.e., sound doctrine). Anyone denying the true

22 *Who is a liar but he who denies that Jesus is the Christ? He is antichrist who denies the Father and the Son.*

23 *Whoever denies the Son does not have the Father either; he who acknowledges the Son has the Father also.*

nature of Christ as presented in the Scripture is an antichrist (see 4:2; 2 Thess. 2:11).

24 *Therefore let that abide in you which you heard from the beginning. If what you heard from the beginning abides in you, you also will abide in the Son and in the Father.*

25 *And this is the promise that He has promised us— eternal life.*

26 *These things I have written to you concerning those who try to deceive you.*

27 *But the anointing which you have received from Him abides in you, and you do not need that anyone teach you; but as the same anointing teaches you concerning all things, and is true, and is not a lie, and just as it has taught you, you will abide in Him.*

heard from the beginning (vv. 24–25)—The gospel that cannot change. Christian truth is fixed and unalterable (Jude 3).

those who try to deceive you (v. 26)—A third characteristic of antichrists is that they try to deceive the faithful (see also 1 Tim. 4:1).

do not need that anyone teach you (v. 27)—John is not denying the importance of gifted teachers in the church (1 Cor. 12:28; Eph. 4:11), but indicates that neither those teachers nor those believers are dependent on human wisdom or the opinions of men for the truth. God's Holy Spirit guards and guides the true believer into the truth.

abide in Him (v. 27)—In response to such deceivers, the task of the genuine believer is to "walk in the truth," i.e., persevere in faithfulness and sound doctrine (see vv. 20–21; 2 John 4; 3 John 4).

1) What is significant about John's statement that he writes in "the last hour" (v. 18)?

_____

_____

_____

2) What does verse 19 say about the perseverance of the saints? What will be true of those who are genuinely born-again?

_____

_____

_____

3) What did John mean by the anointing (v. 20)? Who gets this anointing?

_____

_____

_____

4) How can we discern the presence of an antichrist? What characteristics set true believers apart from the antichrists?

_____

_____

_____

_____

_____

5) What is the promise or reward for those who stay faithful to the truth (v. 27)?

_____

_____

_____

_____

_____

GOING DEEPER

John taught about the Father and the Son. For more insight on this relationship, read John 5:32–38.

32 *There is another who bears witness of Me, and I know that the witness which He witnesses of Me is true.*

33 *You have sent to John, and he has borne witness to the truth.*

34 *Yet I do not receive testimony from man, but I say these things that you may be saved.*

35 *He was the burning and shining lamp, and you were willing for a time to rejoice in his light.*

36 *But I have a greater witness than John's; for the works which the Father has given Me to finish—the very works that I do—bear witness of Me, that the Father has sent Me.*

37 *And the Father Himself, who sent Me, has testified of Me. You have neither heard His voice at any time, nor seen His form.*

38 *But you do not have His word abiding in you, because whom He sent, Him you do not believe.*

10) How does God's Holy Spirit guide believers into the truth (see John 15:26; 16:17)?

_____

_____

_____

_____

_____

_____

Truth for Today

John's love of truth is evident in all his writings. He uses the Greek word for *truth* twenty-five times in his gospel and twenty more times in his epistles. He wrote, "I have no greater joy than to hear that my children walk in truth" (3 John 4 NKJV). His strongest epithet for someone who claimed to be a believer while walking in darkness was to describe the person as "a liar, and the truth is not in him" (1 John 2:4 NKJV). No one in all of Scripture, except the Lord Himself, had more to say extolling the concept of truth.

Reflecting on the Text

11) As believers in Jesus, we have been given the very Spirit of God to guard and guide us (John 16:13; 1 John 2:20), to empower us (Acts 1:8), and to be our Helper (John 14:16). Evaluate the work of the Spirit in your life.

⟶ In what specific situations have you *grieved* the Spirit (Eph. 4:30)?

⟶ How have you *quenched* the Spirit (1 Thess. 5:19)?

⟶ When have you *failed to walk in* the Spirit (Gal. 5:25)?

_____

_____

_____

_____

_____

_____

Exploring the Meaning

6) According to Jesus' own words, how is denying Christ tantamount to also denying the Father? (See also 1 John 2:22.)

_____

_____

_____

_____

_____

_____

7) How is the Holy Spirit like a built-in lie detector (2:20, 27)?

_____

_____

_____

_____

_____

8) What are some "antichrist" attitudes and behaviors that are common in our culture?

_____

_____

_____

_____

9) Define what it means to "abide" in the truth and in Christ (2:24).

_____

_____

_____

_____

_____

24 *Therefore let that abide in you which you heard from the beginning. If what you heard from the beginning abides in you, you also will abide in the Son and in the Father.*

25 *And this is the promise that He has promised us— eternal life.*

26 *These things I have written to you concerning those who try to deceive you.*

27 *But the anointing which you have received from Him abides in you, and you do not need that anyone teach you; but as the same anointing teaches you concerning all things, and is true, and is not a lie, and just as it has taught you, you will abide in Him.*

heard from the beginning (vv. 24–25)—The gospel that cannot change. Christian truth is fixed and unalterable (Jude 3).

those who try to deceive you (v. 26)—A third characteristic of antichrists is that they try to deceive the faithful (see also 1 Tim. 4:1).

do not need that anyone teach you (v. 27)—John is not denying the importance of gifted teachers in the church (1 Cor. 12:28; Eph. 4:11), but indicates that neither those teachers nor those believers are dependent on human wisdom or the opinions of men for the truth. God's Holy Spirit guards and guides the true believer into the truth.

abide in Him (v. 27)—In response to such deceivers, the task of the genuine believer is to "walk in the truth," i.e., persevere in faithfulness and sound doctrine (see vv. 20–21; 2 John 4; 3 John 4).

1) What is significant about John's statement that he writes in "the last hour" (v. 18)?

_____

_____

_____

2) What does verse 19 say about the perseverance of the saints? What will be true of those who are genuinely born-again?

_____

_____

_____

3) What did John mean by the anointing (v. 20)? Who gets this anointing?

_____

_____

_____

4) How can we discern the presence of an antichrist? What characteristics set true believers apart from the antichrists?

_____

_____

_____

_____

_____

5) What is the promise or reward for those who stay faithful to the truth (v. 27)?

_____

_____

_____

_____

_____

GOING DEEPER

John taught about the Father and the Son. For more insight on this relationship, read John 5:32–38.

32 *There is another who bears witness of Me, and I know that the witness which He witnesses of Me is true.*

33 *You have sent to John, and he has borne witness to the truth.*

34 *Yet I do not receive testimony from man, but I say these things that you may be saved.*

35 *He was the burning and shining lamp, and you were willing for a time to rejoice in his light.*

36 *But I have a greater witness than John's; for the works which the Father has given Me to finish—the very works that I do—bear witness of Me, that the Father has sent Me.*

37 *And the Father Himself, who sent Me, has testified of Me. You have neither heard His voice at any time, nor seen His form.*

38 *But you do not have His word abiding in you, because whom He sent, Him you do not believe.*

12) List two specific things you will do this week to abide in the truth and protect yourself from falling into error.

_____

_____

_____

_____

_____

Personal Response

Write out additional reflections, questions you may have, or a prayer.

_____

_____

_____

_____

_____

_____

_____

_____

_____

_____

_____

_____

_____

_____

_____

_____

Additional Notes

~4~
PURITY

DRAWING NEAR

How much do you think about the return of Christ? Do you think it will be during your lifetime? Why or why not?

_____

_____

_____

_____

If Christians lived with a fervent belief in the imminent (at-any-moment) return of Jesus, how would their lives be different?

_____

_____

_____

_____

_____

THE CONTEXT

John turns to the "purifying hope" of every Christian, that is, the return of Christ. John uses this purifying hope to elaborate on the moral test (love and obedience) of a true Christian. The hope of Christ's return has a sanctifying effect on moral behavior. In anticipation of Christ's return and reward, a genuine Christian walks in holiness of life. Those who do not evidence such behavior manifest an unsaved life.

One of John's primary aims is to combat false teachers who are corrupting the fundamentals of the faith. Genuine believers will practice righteousness and love toward fellow believers. John was very concerned that Christians know how to tell the true from the false, the genuine from the artificial, true believers from false ones. He presents tests here to help determine these things.

Keys to the Text

Abide: This means to "remain" or "stay around." (Note: We get our English word *abode*, "home or dwelling place," from this root.) This "remaining" is evidence that salvation has already taken place. The evidence of salvation is continuance in service to Him and in His teaching. The abiding believer is the only legitimate believer. Abiding and believing actually are addressing the same issue of genuine salvation. Whenever John refers to abiding, he is referring to persevering in the faith of salvation, which is evidence of being a true believer.

Unleashing the Text

Read 1 John 2:28–3:24, noting the key words and definitions next to the passage.

1 John 2:28–3:24 (NKJV)

when He appears (v. 28)—This refers especially to the Rapture and gathering of the church (see 1 Cor. 15:51–54; 1 Thess. 4:13–18), and the Judgment Seat of Christ to follow (see 1 Cor. 4:5; 2 Cor. 5:9–10).

confidence . . . not be ashamed before Him (v. 28)—"Confidence" means "outspokenness" or "freedom of speech." Those who are saved will have confidence at Christ's coming because they will be blameless in holiness, based on abiding in Christ (Eph. 5:27. Col. 1:22. 1 Thess. 3:13. 5:23).

everyone who practices righteousness is born of Him (v. 29)—The hope of Christ's return not only sustains faith (v. 28), but makes righteousness a habit.

28 *And now, little children, abide in Him, that when He appears, we may have confidence and not be ashamed before Him at His coming.*

29 *If you know that He is righteous, you know that everyone who practices righteousness is born of Him.*

3:1 *Behold what manner of love the Father has bestowed on us, that we should be called children of God! Therefore the world does not know us, because it did not know Him.*

2 *Beloved, now we are children of God; and it has not yet been revealed what we shall be, but we know that when He is revealed, we shall be like Him, for we shall see Him as He is.*

Therefore the world does not know us (3:1)—The real aliens in the world are not extraterrestrials but Christians. Having been born again and given a new nature of heavenly origin, Christians display a nature and lifestyle like their Savior and heavenly Father—a nature totally foreign (otherworldly) to the unsaved.

now we are children of God (v. 2)—Everyone who exercises genuine saving faith becomes a child of God at the moment of belief (John 1:12; Rom. 8:16; 2 Pet. 1:4), though the truly heavenly, divine life in that person (see Eph. 4:24; Col. 3:10) will not be revealed until Jesus appears.

we shall be like Him (v. 2)—When Christ returns, He shall conform every believer to His image, i.e., His nature. The glorious nature of that conformity defies description, but rest assured that believers will be as close to incarnate deity as humanity can possibly become.

3 *And everyone who has this hope in Him purifies himself, just as He is pure.*

4 *Whoever commits sin also commits lawlessness, and sin is lawlessness.*

5 *And you know that He was manifested to take away our sins, and in Him there is no sin.*

6 *Whoever abides in Him does not sin. Whoever sins has neither seen Him nor known Him.*

7 *Little children, let no one deceive you. He who practices righteousness is righteous, just as He is righteous.*

8 *He who sins is of the devil, for the devil has sinned from the beginning. For this purpose the Son of God was manifested, that He might destroy the works of the devil.*

9 *Whoever has been born of God does not sin, for His seed remains in him; and he cannot sin, because he has been born of God.*

10 *In this the children of God and the children of the devil are manifest: Whoever does not practice*

purifies himself, just as He is pure (v. 3)—Since Christians someday will be like Him, a desire should grow within the Christian to become like Him now.

commits sin (v. 4)—The Greek verb for "commits" conveys the idea of making sin a habitual practice. Although genuine Christians have a sin nature (1:8) and do commit sin, which they in turn need to confess (1:9; 2:1), that is not the unbroken pattern of their lives.

sin is lawlessness (v. 4)—The term "lawlessness" conveys more than transgressing God's law; it means rebellion, i.e., living as if there were no law or ignoring laws that do exist (James 4:17).

He was manifested to take away our sins (v. 5)—Christ died to sanctify (i.e., make holy) the believer (2 Cor. 5:21; Eph. 5:25–27). To sin is contrary to Christ's work of breaking the dominion of sin in the believer's life (Rom. 6:1–15).

does not sin (v. 6)—Like the phrase "commits sin" of verse 4, the sense conveyed here is the idea of habitual, constant sinning.

let no one deceive you (v. 6)—"to be led astray"; accepting what the false teachers were advocating

just as He is righteous (v. 7)—Those who are truly born again reflect the divine nature of the Son; they behave like Him, manifesting the power of His life in them (Gal. 2:20).

of the devil (v. 8)—The phrase gives the source of the false teachers' actions; the term "devil" means "accuser" or "slanderer."

from the beginning (v. 8)—Satan was originally created as perfect and only later rebelled against God (Isa. 14:12–14; Ezek. 24:12–17). John probably means the moment of his rebellion against God, the beginning of his rebellious career.

For this purpose . . . that He might destroy (v. 8)—Christ came to destroy the works of the archsinner, Satan; the devil is still operating, but he has been defeated, and, in Christ, we escape his tyranny. The day will come when all of Satan's activity will cease in the universe and he will be sent to hell forever (Rev. 20:10).

born of God (v. 9)—The new birth (John 3:7). When people become Christians, God makes them new creatures with new natures (2 Cor. 5:17).

remains (v. 9)—conveys the idea of the permanence of the new birth, which cannot be reversed, for those who are truly born-again are permanently transformed into a new creation (2 Cor. 5:17; Gal. 6:15; Eph. 2:10)

he cannot sin (v. 9)—This phrase once again conveys the idea of habitual sinning (see vv. 4, 6).

he who does not love his brother (v. 10)—The false teachers not only had an erroneous view of Christ's nature and displayed disobedience to God's commands, but they also displayed a distinct lack of love for true believers, who rejected their heretical teaching.

we should love one another (v. 11)—Love is not merely an optional duty for someone claiming to be a Christian, but positive proof that one truly has been born again (John 15:12; 1 Pet. 1:22–23).

Cain (v. 12)—Scripture presents Cain outwardly as a God-worshiper who even offered a sacrifice (Gen. 4:3–5). His murderous actions, however, revealed that inwardly he was an enemy of God (see John 8:44).

the world hates you (v. 13)—History is filled with stories of the persecution of the saints by the world (Heb. 11:36–40).

passed from death to life, because we love (v. 14)—Becoming a Christian is a resurrection from death to life and a turning of hate to love (see Gal. 5:6, 22). A lack of love indicates that one is spiritually dead.

abides in death (v. 14)—Someone who is characterized by hate has never experienced the new birth.

He laid down His life for us (v. 16)—This expression is unique to John (John 10:11, 15, 17, 18; 13:37, 38; 15:13) and speaks of divesting oneself of something;

righteousness is not of God, nor is he who does not love his brother.

11 *For this is the message that you heard from the beginning, that we should love one another,*

12 *not as Cain who was of the wicked one and murdered his brother. And why did he murder him? Because his works were evil and his brother's righteous.*

13 *Do not marvel, my brethren, if the world hates you.*

14 *We know that we have passed from death to life, because we love the brethren. He who does not love his brother abides in death.*

15 *Whoever hates his brother is a murderer, and you know that no murderer has eternal life abiding in him.*

16 *By this we know love, because He laid down His life for us. And we also ought to lay down our lives for the brethren.*

17 *But whoever has this world's goods, and sees his brother in need, and shuts up his heart from him, how does the love of God abide in him?*

18 *My little children, let us not love in word or in tongue, but in deed and in truth.*

19 *And by this we know that we are of the truth, and shall assure our hearts before Him.*

20 *For if our heart condemns us, God is greater than our heart, and knows all things.*

21 *Beloved, if our heart does not condemn us, we have confidence toward God.*

22 *And whatever we ask we receive from Him, because we keep His commandments and do those things that are pleasing in His sight.*

Christian love is self-sacrificing and giving. Christ's giving up His life for believers epitomized the true nature of Christian love (John 15:12–13; Phil. 2:5–8; 1 Pet. 2:19–23), and we are called to the same standard.

in word or in tongue . . . in deed and in truth (v. 18)—Love is not sentiment, but deeds.

by this we know (v. 19)—A lifestyle of love in action is the demonstrable proof of salvation (see v. 16).

if our heart condemns us, God is greater (v. 20)—Although Christians may have insecurities and doubts about salvation, God does not condemn them (Rom. 8:10).

confidence toward God (v. 21)—Love banishes self-condemnation and results in confidence.

23 *And this is His commandment: that we should believe on the name of His Son Jesus Christ and love one another, as He gave us commandment.*
24 *Now he who keeps His commandments abides in Him, and He in him. And by this we know that He abides in us, by the Spirit whom He has given us.*

1) What did John suggest will be the experience for those who are not abiding in Christ at the time of His return (2:28)?

_____

_____

_____

_____

_____

2) What idea or truth specifically prompted John's outburst of wonder and praise at the beginning of chapter 3?

_____

_____

_____

_____

_____

3) What did John mean when he said, "the world does not know us" (3:1)? (Hint: See Hebrews 11:13; 1 Peter 1:1; 2:11.)

_____

_____

_____

_____

4) What four reasons are given for why true Christians cannot habitually practice sin (3:4–10)?

_____

_____

_____

_____

_____

5) What did John say about Satan and sin in 3:8?

_____

_____

_____

_____

6) In what ways can we show and "do" love (3:16–23)?

_____

_____

_____

_____

_____

GOING DEEPER

John clearly says that if we are children of God, we will practice righteousness. For more insight, read 1 Peter 1:3, 13–16.

3 *Blessed be the God and Father of our Lord Jesus Christ, who according to His abundant mercy has begotten us again to a living hope through the resurrection of Jesus Christ from the dead . . .*

13 *Therefore gird up the loins of your mind, be sober, and rest your hope fully upon the grace that is to be brought to you at the revelation of Jesus Christ;*

14 *as obedient children, not conforming yourselves to the former lusts, as in your ignorance;*

15 *but as He who called you is holy, you also be holy in all your conduct,*

16 *because it is written, "Be holy, for I am holy."*

EXPLORING THE MEANING

7) What does Peter say about our new nature and new conduct as children of God?

_____

_____

_____

_____

_____

8) Why did John argue that true Christians cannot "practice" sin?

_____

_____

_____

_____

9) What did John mean when he spoke of "children of the devil" (3:10; see also John 8:44)? How does this fit in with the popular notion today that everyone is a "child of God"?

_____

_____

_____

_____

_____

10) How does John use Cain as an example in his letter (3:10–12)?

_____

_____

_____

_____

_____

Truth for Today

Commitment to truth is not enough. Zeal for the truth must be balanced by love for people. Truth without love has no decency; it's just *brutality*. On the other hand, love without truth has no character; it's just *hypocrisy*. Many people place too much emphasis on the love side of the fulcrum. They talk a lot about love and tolerance, but they utterly lack any concern for the truth. Real love "does not rejoice in iniquity, but rejoices in the truth" (1 Cor. 13:6 NKJV). On the other hand, there are many who have all their theological ducks in a row and know their doctrine but are unloving and self-exalting. They are left with truth as cold facts, stifling and unattractive. Their lack of love cripples the power of the truth they profess to revere.

The truly godly person must cultivate both virtues in equal proportions. If you could wish for anything in your sanctification, wish for that. If you pursue anything in the spiritual realm, pursue a perfect balance of truth and love. Know the truth, and uphold it in love.

Reflecting on the Text

11) Review 1 John 3:1–3, as though reading it for the first time. Spend a few minutes pondering this rich paragraph. Then record your impressions.

_____

_____

_____

_____

_____

_____

_____

_____

_____

_____

_____

_____

12) John reminds us that real love is not sentimental and it is more than lip service (3:18). In the chart below, list some tangible expressions of love that you can demonstrate this week:

Person to Whom I Will Show Love	How I Will Show Love

PERSONAL RESPONSE

Write out additional reflections, questions you may have, or a prayer.

Additional Notes

TRUE AND FALSE DOCTRINE

DRAWING NEAR

Have you ever talked with someone from a non-Christian religious cult? If so, what was the conversation like? What topics did you discuss?

_____

_____

_____

_____

_____

How do you discern if a religious system/teacher is sound or bogus?

_____

_____

_____

_____

THE CONTEXT

Good teachers know that one of the most effective ways students learn is by repetition. Astute preachers recognize the power of "driving home" a truth by restating it in different terms. John makes use of this method in chapter 4, where he begins a third pass over the bedrock basics of the faith.

John turns again to the importance of belief in God's truth. He focuses once more on the doctrinal test and emphasizes the need to obey sound teaching. Scripture presents stern warnings against false doctrine. Ever since the temptation of Eve, Satan has sought to distort and deny God's Word. He is the ultimate demonic source behind all false teachers and false doctrine. In this section, John gives two tests to determine truth from error and false teachers from true teachers.

KEYS TO THE TEXT

Test the Spirits: This term means to "test or try, examine or interpret." To "test" is a metallurgist's term used for assaying metals to determine their purity and value. In the New Testament, Christians are urged to test any teaching with a view to approving or disapproving it, rigorously comparing any teaching to the Scripture. Believers are to be discerning, to examine the preached word carefully and soberly. Whatever is found to be in accordance with God's revelation is to be wholeheartedly embraced. If it's not, then it is false and should be shunned.

UNLEASHING THE TEXT

Read 1 John 4:1–6, noting the key words and definitions next to the passage.

1 John 4:1–6 (NKJV)

do not believe every spirit (v. 1)—The mention of the Holy Spirit in 3:24 prompts John to inform his readers that those other spirits exist, i.e., demonic spirits, who produce false prophets and false teachers to propagate their false doctrine.

the spirits . . . many false prophets (v. 1)—By juxtaposing "spirits" with "false prophets" John reminds his readers that behind human teachers who propagate false doctrine and error are demons inspired by Satan. Human false prophets and teachers are the physical expressions of demonic, spiritual sources (Matt. 7:15; Mark 13:22).

1 Beloved, do not believe every spirit, but test the spirits, whether they are of God; because many false prophets have gone out into the world.

2 By this you know the Spirit of God: Every spirit that confesses that Jesus Christ has come in the flesh is of God,

3 and every spirit that does not confess that Jesus Christ has come in the flesh is not of God. And this is the spirit of the Antichrist, which you have heard was coming, and is now already in the world.

4 You are of God, little children, and have overcome them, because He who is in you is greater than he who is in the world.

By this you know the Spirit of God (v. 2)—a measuring stick to determine whether the propagator of the message is a demon spirit or the Holy Spirit

Jesus Christ has come in the flesh (v. 2)—The Greek construction does not mean that they confess Christ as having come to earth, but that they confess that He came in the flesh to the earth, i.e., His human body was physically real.

the spirit of the Antichrist (v. 3)—These false teachers who denied the true nature of the Son are to be identified among the antichrists in 2:28–29. The final Antichrist will not represent a new concept, but will be the ultimate embodiment of all the antichrist spirits that have perverted truth and propagated satanic lies since the beginning.

He who is in you is greater (v. 4)—Believers need to be aware and alert to false teaching, but not afraid of it, since those who have experienced the new birth with its indwelling of the Holy Spirit have a built-in check against false teaching. Furthermore, not even Satan's hosts with their perversions can take them out of the Lord's hand.

5 *They are of the world. Therefore they speak as of the world, and the world hears them.*

6 *We are of God. He who knows God hears us; he who is not of God does not hear us. By this we know the spirit of truth and the spirit of error.*

they speak as of the world . . . He who knows God hears us (vv. 5–6)—They speak God's Word, following apostolic doctrine.

By this we know the spirit of truth and the spirit of error (v. 6)—The Old Testament and New Testament are the sole standards by which all teaching is to be tested. In contrast, demonically inspired teachers either reject the teaching of God's Word or add elements to it (2 Cor. 4:2; Rev. 22:18–19).

1) What did John mean when he urged his readers to "test the spirits" (v. 1)?

_____

_____

_____

_____

_____

2) What is the first test of a true teacher of God (v. 2)?

_____

_____

_____

_____

_____

3) According to John, who or what motivates false teachers?

_____

_____

_____

_____

_____

4) What is the encouraging promise of verse 4? To whom is John referring?

_____

_____

_____

_____

_____

_____

5) What is the second test of a true teacher (vv. 5–6)?

_____

_____

_____

_____

_____

_____

_____

GOING DEEPER

The apostle Paul also warned the early Christians about false teaching. Read
1 Thessalonians 5:20–22 and Acts 20:28–32.

1 Thess. 5:20 *Do not despise prophecies.*

21 Test all things; hold fast what is good.

22 Abstain from every form of evil.

Acts 20:28 *Therefore take heed to yourselves and to all the flock, among which
the Holy Spirit has made you overseers, to shepherd the church of
God which He purchased with His own blood.*

*29 For I know this, that after my departure savage wolves will come in
among you, not sparing the flock.*

*30 Also from among yourselves men will rise up, speaking perverse
things, to draw away the disciples after themselves.*

*31 Therefore watch, and remember that for three years I did not cease to
warn everyone night and day with tears.*

*32 So now, brethren, I commend you to God and to the word of His
grace, which is able to build you up and give you an inheritance
among all those who are sanctified.*

Exploring the Meaning

6) According to Paul, what are some ways to combat false teaching? What part does God's Word play?

_____

_____

_____

_____

_____

_____

7) Read Acts 17:10–11. Why were the Berean Christians commended?

_____

_____

_____

_____

_____

8) Why is it absolutely essential that teachers in the church embrace the full humanity and deity of Christ?

_____

_____

_____

_____

9) How did John define the "spirit of Antichrist" (v. 3)?

_____

_____

_____

_____

_____

10) Why did John insist that Christians do not need to fear the false teachers who were motivated by the spirit of the Antichrist?

_____

_____

_____

_____

Truth for Today

An important gift for the protection of the church is that of discernment, the distinguishing of spirits. Those with the gift of discernment are the Holy Spirit's inspectors, His counterfeit experts to whom He gives special insight and understanding. The gift was especially valuable in the early church because the New Testament had not been completed. False teaching can be judged by comparing it with Scripture, but false spirits can be judged only by the true Spirit's gift of discernment.

All Christians should judge carefully what they hear and read, and "test the spirits, [to see] whether they are from God" (1 John 4:1 NKJV). That is what the God-fearing Jews of Berea did when they first heard the gospel from Paul (Acts 17:11). They tested Paul's word against what they knew of God's Word, and because the two matched, they believed that what he preached was from God. Some ideas that on the surface _seem_ scriptural are actually clever counterfeits that would deceive most believers. It is not always easy to know which are true and which are not. Most often they are a mixture. Counterfeit teachers used by Satan usually have some truth in what they say. It is the ministry of those with the gift of discernment to help separate the wheat from the chaff.

Reflecting on the Text

11) How careful are you about examining the messages and sermons you hear at church, on TV, on the radio, or via the Internet? How can you guard against buying into wrong ideas about God, faith, and the spiritual life?

_____

_____

_____

_____

12) Reflect on the truth in 1 John 4:4. What difference does it make in your life knowing that God is greater than all other powers?

_____

_____

_____

_____

_____

PERSONAL RESPONSE

Write out additional reflections, questions you may have, or a prayer.

_____

_____

_____

_____

_____

_____

_____

_____

_____

_____

_____

_____

_____

_____

_____

_____

ADDITIONAL NOTES

~6~
LOVE

1 John 4:7–21

DRAWING NEAR

How is *love* depicted in television shows and movies? Considering our culture's high divorce rate, how do most people seem to define marital love?

When in your life have you been the most overwhelmed by the reality of God's love for you?

THE CONTEXT

It is clear from the gospel accounts that, early in life, John was capable of behaving in the most sectarian, narrow-minded, unbending, reckless, and impetuous fashion. He was volatile. He was brash. He was aggressive. But John aged well. Under the control of the Holy Spirit, his liabilities were exchanged for assets. Compare the young disciple with the aged patriarch, and you'll see that as he matured, his areas of greatest weakness developed into his greatest strengths. He's an amazing example of what should happen to us as we grow in Christ— allowing the Lord's strength to be made perfect in our weakness. When we think of the apostle John today, we usually think of a tenderhearted, elderly apostle. As the elder statesman of the church near the end of the first century, he was universally beloved and respected for his devotion to Christ and his great love for the saints worldwide. That is precisely why he earned the epithet "apostle of love."

John states that genuine Christians will love in radical ways. This section constitutes one long unit describing what perfect love is and that it is available to all. John lists five reasons true Christians live by love.

Christians love because God is the essence of love, in order to follow the supreme example of God's sacrificial love in sending His Son for us, because love is the heart of Christian witness, because love is the Christian's assurance, and because love is the Christian's confidence in judgment.

Love originated in God, it was manifested in His Son, and now it is demonstrated in His people. One cannot love God without first loving his fellow believer. John reminds us that a claim to love God is a delusion if not accompanied by unselfish love for other Christians.

Keys to the Text

Love: John uses the Greek word *agape,* one of the rarest words in ancient Greek literature, but one of the most common in the New Testament. Unlike our English word for *love,* it never refers to romantic or sexual love (*eros,* which does not appear in the New Testament). It does not mean friendship or brotherly love (*philia).* The supreme measure and example of *agape* love is God's love. "God so loved the world that He gave His only begotten Son" (John 3:16 NKJV). Love is, above all, sacrificial. It is sacrifice of self for the sake of others, even for others who may care nothing at all for us and who may even hate us. It is not a feeling but a determined act of will, which always results in acts of self-giving.

Propitiation: This term means "appeasement" or "satisfaction." The sacrifice of Jesus on the cross satisfied the demands of God's holiness for the punishment of sin (see Rom. 1:18; 2 Cor. 5:21). Hence Jesus propitiated or satisfied God. Hebrews 9:5 translates a form of the word *propitiation* as "the mercy seat." Christ literally became our mercy seat, like the one in the Holy of Holies, where the high priest splattered the blood of the sacrifice on the Day of Atonement (see Lev. 16:15).

Unleashing the Text

Read 1 John 4:7–21, noting the key words and definitions next to the passage.

1 John 4:7–21 (NKJV)

7 Beloved, let us love one another, for love is of God; and everyone who loves is born of God and knows God.

8 He who does not love does not know God, for God is love.

9 In this the love of God was manifested toward us, that God has sent His only begotten Son into the world, that we might live through Him.

10 In this is love, not that we loved God, but that He loved us and sent His Son to be the propitiation for our sins.

11 Beloved, if God so loved us, we also ought to love one another.

12 No one has seen God at any time. If we love one another, God abides in us, and His love has been perfected in us.

13 By this we know that we abide in Him, and He in us, because He has given us of His Spirit.

14 And we have seen and testify that the Father has sent the Son as Savior of the world.

15 Whoever confesses that Jesus is the Son of God, God abides in him, and he in God.

16 And we have known and believed the love that God has for us. God is love, and he who abides in love abides in God, and God in him.

17 Love has been perfected among us in this: that we may have boldness in the day of judgment; because as He is, so are we in this world.

let us love one another (v. 7)—This phrase is the key to the entire section (see v. 21). It conveys the idea of making sure that love is a habitual practice.

everyone who loves is born of God (v. 7)—Those who are born again receive God's nature. Since God's nature exhibits love as a chief characteristic (see v. 8), God's children will also reflect that love.

He who does not love does not know God (v. 8)—Someone may profess to be a Christian but only those who display love like their heavenly Father actually possess His Divine nature and are truly born-again.

the love of God was manifested (v. 9)—The judgment of sin on the cross was the supreme example of God's love, for He poured out His wrath on His beloved Son in place of sinners.

only begotten (v. 9)—Over half of the New Testament's uses of this term are by John. He always uses it of Christ to picture His unique relationship to the Father, His preexistence, and His distinctness from creation. The term emphasizes the uniqueness of Christ, as the only one of His kind.

we also ought (v. 11)—God's sending His Son obligates Christians to follow this pattern of sacrificial love.

No one has seen God (v. 12)—Nobody can see God's love since it is invisible and Jesus is no longer in the world to manifest the love of God. The church is the only remaining demonstration of God's love in this age.

whoever confesses (v. 15)—This refers to the doctrinal test (see vv. 1–6; 1:1–4; 2:23).

Love . . . perfected among us (v. 17)—John is not suggesting sinless perfection, but mature love marked by confidence in the face of judgment.

as He is, so are we (v. 17)—Jesus was God's Son in whom He was well pleased on earth. We also are God's children (3:11) and the objects of His gracious goodness. If Jesus called God Father, so may we, since we are accepted in the Beloved (Eph. 1:6).

18 *There is no fear in love; but perfect love casts out fear, because fear involves torment. But he who fears has not been made perfect in love.*

19 *We love Him because He first loved us.*

20 *If someone says, "I love God," and hates his brother, he is a liar; for he who does not love his brother whom he has seen, how can he love God whom he has not seen?*

21 *And this commandment we have from Him: that he who loves God must love his brother also.*

1) Where does love come from, and what are the ramifications of this for those who claim to be Christians?

_____

_____

_____

_____

_____

2) How has God demonstrated His love?

_____

_____

_____

_____

_____

3) Based on verse 12, why is it imperative that Christians be marked by God's love?

_____

_____

_____

_____

_____

_____

4) In what ways did John insist that love leads to confidence and not fear?

_____

_____

_____

_____

_____

_____

5) How did John expose the lies we often live out (vv. 20–21)? How is love to be expressed?

_____

_____

_____

_____

_____

_____

Going Deeper

John learned about love from the best teacher of all: Jesus. To see what Jesus taught, read John 15:9–17.

9   *"As the Father loved Me, I also have loved you; abide in My love.*

10 *If you keep My commandments, you will abide in My love, just as I have kept My Father's commandments and abide in His love.*

11 *"These things I have spoken to you, that My joy may remain in you, and that your joy may be full.*

12 *This is My commandment, that you love one another as I have loved you.*

13 *Greater love has no one than this, than to lay down one's life for his friends.*

14 *You are My friends if you do whatever I command you.*

15 *No longer do I call you servants, for a servant does not know what his master is doing; but I have called you friends, for all things that I heard from My Father I have made known to you.*

16 *You did not choose Me, but I chose you and appointed you that you should go and bear fruit, and that your fruit should remain, that whatever you ask the Father in My name He may give you.*

17 *These things I command you, that you love one another."*

Exploring the Meaning

6) According to Jesus, how can we abide in His love?

_____

_____

_____

_____

_____

7) How does Jesus define the kind of love He is talking about?

_____

_____

_____

_____

8) According to John, why is it impossible to love God and hate our neighbor at the same time (vv. 20–21)?

_____

_____

_____

_____

9) What "safeguards" did John include in his description of love, to keep his readers from thinking of love as a nebulous, fuzzy, vague, sentimental feeling?

_____

_____

_____

_____

_____

10) Based on 1 John 4:7–21, what does a God-honoring love look like in a believer's life?

_____

_____

_____

_____

_____

_____

Truth for Today

Love is so much an absolute of the Christian life that Jesus said to those disciples, "A new commandment I give to you, that you love one another; as I have loved you, that you also love one another. By this all will know that you are My disciples, if you have love for one another" (John 13:34–35 NKJV). Jesus left no doubt that love—*agape* love, self-sacrificing love—is the supreme mark of discipleship to Him. He both taught it and demonstrated it.

Jesus' teaching can be summarized in five keys to loving: (1) Love is commanded; (2) love is already possessed by Christians; (3) love is the norm of Christian living; (4) love is the work of the Spirit; and (5) love must be practiced to be genuine. When we stray from the Source of love, it is impossible to be loving. Self-giving love, love that demands something of us, love that is more concerned with giving than receiving, is as rare in much of the church today as it was in the ancient church.

Reflecting on the Text

11) How do you apply in your life the statement "We love because He first loved us"?

_____

_____

_____

_____

_____

12) A failure to see God in His holiness can breed irreverence. A failure to grasp God's grace and love can lead to unhealthy fear. In your own relationship with God, are you motivated more by love or fear? Why? What can you do to find a healthy balance?

_____

_____

_____

_____

_____

PERSONAL RESPONSE

Write out additional reflections, questions you may have, or a prayer.

_____

_____

_____

_____

_____

_____

_____

_____

_____

_____

_____

_____

_____

_____

_____

7

THE VICTORIOUS LIFE

1 John 5:1–5

DRAWING NEAR

Looking back over your life, think for a few moments about any small "victories" you've had. List them below:

⟶ Athletic accomplishments

⟶ Academic achievements

⟶ Marital milestones

⟶ Career triumphs

_____

_____

_____

_____

_____

_____

To what do you attribute those victories? (Don't be cocky or overly modest!)

_____

_____

_____

_____

THE CONTEXT

The way John wrote was a reflection of his personality. Truth was his passion, and he seemed to bend over backwards not to make it fuzzy. In his final "spiral" (John's literary device for returning to his main themes), John introduces the subject of the victorious life. This is one of his fundamental tests for genuine fellowship.

While the Bible uses many terms to describe Christians, John highlights one particular term in this chapter: the *overcomer*. Of the twenty-four times the word *overcome* occurs in the New Testament, John uses it twenty-one times (see also Rev. 2:7, 11, 17; 2:26; 3:5, 12, 21). Several different forms of this term appear in these verses to emphasize the victorious nature of the believer. In these five verses, John weaves faith, love, and obedience all together inextricably. They exist mutually in a dynamic relationship. The genuine proof of love is obedience, and the genuine proof of faith is love.

KEYS TO THE TEXT

Overcome: This term means to overpower or triumph. The noun form, *overcomer*, comes from a Greek word meaning "to conquer," "to have victory," "to have superiority," or "conquering power." John clearly defines who these overcomers are: all who believe that Jesus is God's Son. The words convey a genuine superiority that leads to overwhelming success. The victory is demonstrable; it involves overthrowing an enemy so that the victory is seen by all. Jesus used this word to describe Himself (John 16:33). Because of believers' union with Christ, they, too, partake in His victory (Rom. 8:37; 2 Cor. 2:14). The word *overcome* in the original language communicates the truth that the believer has continual victory over the world.

UNLEASHING THE TEXT

Read 1 John 5:1–5, noting the key words and definitions next to the passage.

1 John 5:1–5 (NKJV)

Whoever believes (v. 1)—Saving faith is the first characteristic of an overcomer. The term "believes" conveys the idea of continuing faith, making the point that the mark of genuine believers is that they continue in faith throughout their lives.

1 *Whoever believes that Jesus is the Christ is born of God, and everyone who loves Him who begot also loves him who is begotten of Him.*

Jesus is the Christ (v. 1)—The object of the believer's faith is Jesus, particularly that He is the promised Messiah or "Anointed One" whom God sent to be the Savior from sin.

born of God (v. 1)—This is a reference to the new birth and is the same word that Jesus used in John 3:7. The tense of the Greek verb indicates that ongoing faith is the result of the new birth and, therefore, the evidence of the new birth.

everyone who loves Him who begot also loves him who is begotten of Him (v. 1)—Love is the second characteristic of the overcomer. The overcomer not only believes in God, but loves both God and fellow believers. The moral test is again in view.

2 By this we know that we love the children of God, when we love God and keep His commandments.

3 For this is the love of God, that we keep His commandments. And His commandments are not burdensome.

4 For whatever is born of God overcomes the world. And this is the victory that has overcome the world—our faith.

5 Who is he who overcomes the world, but he who believes that Jesus is the Son of God?

keep His commandments (vv. 2, 3)—Obedience is the third characteristic of an overcomer. The word "keep" conveys the idea of constant obedience (see John 8:31–32; 14:15, 21; 15:10).

His commandments are not burdensome (v. 3)—For example, in contrast to the burdensome, man-made religious traditions of the Jewish leaders (Matt. 23:4), the yoke of Jesus is easy and the burden light (11:30).

the world (vv. 4–5)—Satan's worldwide system of deception and wickedness. Through Christ and His provision of salvation, the believer is a victor (v. 5) over the invisible system of demonic and human evil that Satan operates. John repeats the reference to overcoming the world three times in order to emphasize its importance.

our faith . . . he who believes (vv. 4–5)—Faith in Jesus Christ and dedication of one's life to Him make one an overcomer. John repeats the truth for emphasis.

1) First John 5:1 lists two characteristics of an overcomer. What are they?

_____

_____

_____

_____

2) There is a third characteristic of an overcomer (vv. 2–3). What is it?

_____

_____

_____

3) Looking back over this short passage, what terms and phrases did John repeat? Why this repetition?

_____

_____

_____

_____

4) What did John mean by his statement that God's commands are not "burdensome" (v. 3)?

_____

_____

_____

_____

_____

5) According to John, what is the way to become an overcomer?

_____

_____

_____

_____

_____

GOING DEEPER

We can overcome the world because of the authority of Christ. Read what Jesus taught in John 16:33–17:5.

> 33 *"These things I have spoken to you, that in Me you may have peace. In the world you will have tribulation; but be of good cheer, I have overcome the world."*
>
> 17:1 *Jesus spoke these words, lifted up His eyes to heaven, and said: "Father, the hour has come. Glorify Your Son, that Your Son also may glorify You,*
>
> 2 *as You have given Him authority over all flesh, that He should give eternal life to as many as You have given Him.*
>
> 3 *And this is eternal life, that they may know You, the only true God, and Jesus Christ whom You have sent.*
>
> 4 *I have glorified You on the earth. I have finished the work which You have given Me to do.*
>
> 5 *And now, O Father, glorify Me together with Yourself, with the glory which I had with You before the world was."*

Exploring the Meaning

6) Why was Jesus so confident that He had overcome the world?

_____

_____

_____

_____

_____

_____

7) What further light does Jesus' teaching above shed on John's teaching in 5:1, 5?

_____

_____

_____

_____

8) Did John suggest that all believers are overcomers, or only a few "super Christians"? How do you know?

_____

_____

_____

_____

9) What is the difference between saving faith and intellectual belief?

_____

_____

_____

_____

TRUTH FOR TODAY

When I was a boy, I played in various sports programs. I remember many boys with little or no athletic ability who would try out for these teams. Every once in a while, a coach would feel sorry for such a boy and place him on the team in spite of his performance. He would give the boy a uniform to make him feel that he was a part of the team, even though he would never let the boy play in a game.

Fortunately, the opposite is true in the Christian life. The Lord doesn't place us on the team just so we can sit on the bench. He intends to send us into the game. It is His grace that calls us to salvation, and it is His will that sends us into the world to witness for Him. We are all like the boy who had no ability. God graciously puts us on the team, not because of our own ability, but purely by His sovereign grace. And He gives us the ability to play the game victoriously. So get in the game and give thanks for the holy privilege of serving Jesus Christ.

REFLECTING ON THE TEXT

10) Would you describe most of the Christians you know as "victorious overcomers"? Why or why not?

_____

_____

_____

_____

_____

_____

11) Do you really have faith in and believe that Jesus is the Son of God? Why?

_____

_____

_____

_____

_____

_____

12) It is often said that the children of God have three great enemies. What steps will you take to "overcome" in the following areas?

⁓ The "world"

⁓ The "flesh"

⁓ The "devil"

_____

_____

_____

_____

_____

_____

PERSONAL RESPONSE

Write out additional reflections, questions you may have, or a prayer.

_____

_____

_____

_____

_____

_____

_____

_____

_____

_____

_____

_____

_____

_____

Additional Notes

8

THE TESTIMONY OF GOD

DRAWING NEAR

Have you ever been a witness in a court case or a witness to an auto accident? If so, describe that experience.

_____

_____

_____

_____

How would you define what it means to be a "witness" for Jesus Christ?

_____

_____

_____

_____

THE CONTEXT

The apostle John, advanced in years, wrote his first epistle to confront and refute the heretical notions of a growing number of false teachers who had infiltrated the church. These infidels advocated an early form of Gnosticism, a philosophy that denied the true humanity of Christ and prized the intellectual acquisition of spiritual secret "knowledge" over a practical lifestyle of holiness and obedience to Jesus' teachings.

As part of his final exhortation to the flock of saints that was being bombarded by these heretical teachings, John reminded his readers of the witness of God for Christ. The previous passage described overcomers as those who believed in Jesus as Lord and Savior. Here, John presents God's own testimony to confirm that Jesus is the Christ. He gives two kinds of testimony: external and internal. The term *witness* is the dominant theme of this section. The passage concerns the witness, or testimony, of God and the Spirit regarding the great truth of the deity of Jesus Christ.

KEYS TO THE TEXT

Bears Witness: The verb "witness" comes from the Greek word, *martureo*, and means "to testify, to give testimony, to speak well of, or to vouch for." We get our English word *martyr* from this Greek term. Both the verb "bear witness" and the noun "testimony" come from the same Greek word and are used a total of nine times in this short section. The basic meaning is "someone who has personal and immediate knowledge of something."

UNLEASHING THE TEXT

Read 1 John 5:6–12, noting the key words and definitions next to the passage.

water and blood (v. 6)—Water and the blood refer to Jesus' baptism (water) and death (blood) and constitute external, objective witnesses to who Jesus Christ is.

the Spirit is truth (v. 6)—John no longer stresses apostolic testimony (1:1–4; 4:14) but writes of the testimony of God that comes through the Holy Spirit. Since the Spirit of God cannot lie, His testimony is sure.

three that bear witness (v. 7)—The Old Testament law required "the testimony of two or three witnesses" to establish the truth of a particular matter (Deut. 17:6; 19:15; John 8:17–18).

1 John 5:6–12 (NKJV)

6 *This is He who came by water and blood—Jesus Christ; not only by water, but by water and blood. And it is the Spirit who bears witness, because the Spirit is truth.*

7 *For there are three that bear witness in heaven: the Father, the Word, and the Holy Spirit; and these three are one.*

8 *And there are three that bear witness on earth: the Spirit, the water, and the blood; and these three agree as one.*

9 *If we receive the witness of men, the witness of God is greater; for this is the witness of God which He has testified of His Son.*

in heaven: the Father, the Word, and the Holy Spirit . . . three that bear witness on earth (vv. 7–8)—These words are a direct reference to the Trinity, and what they say is accurate. External manuscript evidence, however, is against their being in the original epistle. They do not appear in any Greek manuscripts dated before about the tenth century AD. No Greek or Latin Father, even those involved in Trinitarian controversies, quote them; no ancient version except the Latin records them (not the Old Latin in its early form or the Vulgate). Internal evidence also militates against their presence, since they disrupt the sense of the writer's thoughts. Most likely, the words were added much later to the text. There is no verse in Scripture that so explicitly states the obvious reality of the Trinity, although many passages imply it strongly (see 2 Cor. 13:14).

the Spirit, the water, and the blood (v. 8)—At the baptism of Jesus, the Father and the Spirit testified to the Son (see Matt. 3:16–17). The death of Jesus Christ also witnessed to who He was (Matt. 27:54; Heb. 9:14). The Holy Spirit testified throughout Jesus' life as to His identity (Mark 1:12; Luke 1:35; Acts 10:38).

10 *He who believes in the Son of God has the witness in himself; he who does not believe God has made Him a liar, because he has not believed the testimony that God has given of His Son.*

11 *And this is the testimony: that God has given us eternal life, and this life is in His Son.*

12 *He who has the Son has life; he who does not have the Son of God does not have life.*

has the witness in himself (v. 10)—John writes of the internal subjective witness to the Son within the believer's heart (Rom. 8:15–16; Gal. 4:6).

made Him a liar (v. 10)—If someone refuses the testimony of God regarding His Son, such rejection is the ultimate form of blasphemy, for it is tantamount to calling God a liar (Titus 1:2; Heb. 6:18).

eternal life . . . in His Son (v. 11)—Life is only in Christ; it is impossible to have it without Him.

1) The false teachers of John's day asserted that a "Christ-spirit" departed from the man Jesus just prior to His death on the cross. How would John's comments about "water and blood" in verse 6 refute this charge?

_____

_____

_____

_____

2) How did John describe the Holy Spirit in this short passage?

_____

_____

_____

_____

3) What three witnesses did John cite as being in agreement about the Son of God?

_____

_____

_____

_____

4) According to John, to refuse to believe in Jesus is tantamount to calling God what (v. 10)?

_____

_____

_____

_____

_____

5) What do verses 11 and 12 teach about eternal life?

_____

_____

_____

_____

_____

Going Deeper

John had witnessed Jesus' glory and heard God's testimony with his own ears. Read Matthew 17:1–7.

1 *Now after six days Jesus took Peter, James, and John his brother, led them up on a high mountain by themselves;*

2 *and He was transfigured before them. His face shone like the sun, and His clothes became as white as the light.*

3 *And behold, Moses and Elijah appeared to them, talking with Him.*

4 *Then Peter answered and said to Jesus, "Lord, it is good for us to be here; if You wish, let us make here three tabernacles: one for You, one for Moses, and one for Elijah."*

5 *While he was still speaking, behold, a bright cloud overshadowed them; and suddenly a voice came out of the cloud, saying, "This is My beloved Son, in whom I am well pleased. Hear Him!"*

6 *And when the disciples heard it, they fell on their faces and were greatly afraid.*

7 *But Jesus came and touched them and said, "Arise, and do not be afraid."*

EXPLORING THE MEANING

6) What does Matthew's account of the transfiguration of Christ reveal and confirm about Jesus' identity?

_____

_____

_____

_____

_____

7) When it comes to Christ's identity, why is God's testimony (1 John 5:9) greater than man's testimony (see 1:1–4)?

_____

_____

_____

_____

_____

8) Why does John stress that there are "three witnesses" (vv. 7–8)? Why is this significant?

_____

_____

_____

_____

_____

TRUTH FOR TODAY

Jesus Christ had to be more than a man; He also had to be God. If Jesus were only a man, even the best of men, He could not have saved believers from their sin. If He were even the right man from the seed of David, but not God, He could not have withstood the punishment of God the Father at the cross and risen from the dead. He could not have overcome Satan, and the world would have been conquered.

If there was ever any question that Jesus was the Son of God, His resurrection from the dead should end it. He had to be man to reach us, but He had to be God to lift us up. When God raised Christ from the dead, He affirmed that what He said was true. As clearly as the horizon divides the earth from the sky, so the resurrection divides Jesus from the rest of humanity. Jesus Christ is God in human flesh.

REFLECTING ON THE TEXT

9) How does the death of Christ also "testify" as to the identity of the Son of God (see Matt. 27:54)?

_____

_____

_____

_____

10) How could you use 1 John 5:11–12 to share with others in very simple terms what it means to be a Christian? What is the "good news" in these verses?

_____

_____

_____

_____

11) Remember, 1 John 5:6–12 is a study about "witnessing"—all the different voices (human and divine) and all the various facts (historical and theological) that form a single chorus to say clearly and loudly, "Jesus is the Christ, the Savior of the world. Trust only in Him." As you conclude this lesson, ask the Spirit of God to search your heart. Is your life adding to this glorious chorus or detracting from it? How are you witnessing to the reality of the Lordship of Christ in your daily attitudes and behavior?

_____

_____

_____

_____

Personal Response

Write out additional reflections, questions you may have, or a prayer.

_____

_____

_____

_____

_____

_____

_____

_____

_____

_____

_____

_____

_____

_____

_____

_____

_____

_____

_____

_____

_____

_____

_____

_____

_____

_____

_____

ADDITIONAL NOTES

～9～
CHRISTIAN CERTAINTIES

1 John 5:13–21

DRAWING NEAR

The apostle John was absolutely certain about the truth of the gospel. But for us, there is a big difference between wondering if a thing is true and being absolutely convinced. Just for fun, go through the following list and record your "certainty level" next to each item.

	No way!	Remote chance	50–50	Inclined to believe	No doubt!
Lee Harvey Oswald acted alone in shooting JFK.	1 2	3 4	5 6	7 8	9 10
UFOs and aliens exist.	1 2	3 4	5 6	7 8	9 10
Scientists will eventually clone people.	1 2	3 4	5 6	7 8	9 10
Researchers will find a cure for cancer.	1 2	3 4	5 6	7 8	9 10
Christ will return in my lifetime.	1 2	3 4	5 6	7 8	9 10
Terrorists will acquire and use weapons of mass destruction.	1 2	3 4	5 6	7 8	9 10
Spanking children "scars" them emotionally.	1 2	3 4	5 6	7 8	9 10
Global warming is a real phenomenon.	1 2	3 4	5 6	7 8	9 10

The Context

Concerned about a plethora of false teachers and their destructive messages, the apostle John sat down and penned this brilliant letter summarizing the fundamentals of Christian faith. Specifically, he gave his readers a self-test for determining the genuineness of a teacher, a message, or an individual's claim of salvation. True faith, John argued, rests on a foundation of doctrinal and moral purity. No one can claim to belong to God or be commissioned by God unless his or her life is marked by orthodox beliefs that result in obedient behavior motivated by love.

God never meant for His children to live in the shadowlands of uncertainty and doubt. He wants us to be sure of where we stand. John accentuates this divine concern for certainty by using the word "know" seven times in this brief final section. John concludes his first epistle with five Christian certainties: the assurance of eternal life (5:13), the promise of answered prayer (5:14–17), the guarantee of victory over sin and Satan (5:18), the pledge that Christians belong to God (5:19), and the certainty that Jesus Christ is the true God (5:20). The greatest certainty of all, the Incarnation, guarantees the certainty of the rest. This is the doctrinal foundation on which we can build our lives.

Keys to the Text

Sin: Literally, "to miss the mark." John speaks of a kind of sin one can recover from, and another kind of sin from which one cannot recover. John's readers, unlike readers today, apparently understood the difference between these two kinds of sin. The overall teaching of this epistle suggests that those who denied the Christian community (2:18–19) to follow heretical, "antichrist" teachings were irrecoverable. Their rebellion and denial of Jesus' true identity (4:1–3) leads to unrepentant sin. In the end, their sin produces spiritual death.

Unleashing the Text

Read 1 John 5:13–21, noting the key words and definitions next to the passage.

1 John 5:13–21 (NKJV)

13 *These things I have written to you who believe in the name of the Son of God, that you may know that you have eternal life, and that you may continue to believe in the name of the Son of God.*

14 *Now this is the confidence that we have in Him, that if we ask anything according to His will, He hears us.*

15 *And if we know that He hears us, whatever we ask, we know that we have the petitions that we have asked of Him.*

16 *If anyone sees his brother sinning a sin which does not lead to death, he will ask, and He will give him life for those who commit sin not leading to death. There is sin leading to death. I do not say that he should pray about that.*

17 *All unrighteousness is sin, and there is sin not leading to death.*

18 *We know that whoever is born of God does not sin; but he who has been born of God keeps himself, and the wicked one does not touch him.*

19 *We know that we are of God, and the whole world lies under the sway of the wicked one.*

These things (v. 13)—This has reference to all that John has written in his letter.

that you may know that you have eternal life (v. 13)—While John wrote his gospel to bring unbelievers to faith (John 20:31), he wrote this epistle to give believers confidence that they possessed eternal life.

eternal life (v. 13)—Refers not primarily to a period of time but to a Person (v. 20; John 17:3). Eternal life is possessing Jesus Christ's nature and having a relationship with Him (as in vv. 11, 12).

confidence (v. 14)—Christians can know with absolute confidence that God answers prayer when they approach the throne of grace (Heb. 4:14).

according to His will (v. 14)—A strategic key to answered prayer. To pray according to God's will is to pray in accord with what He would want, not what we would desire or insist that He do for us (John 14:13–14).

He hears us (v. 14)—The word "hear" signifies that God always hears the prayers of His children (Ps. 34:15–17), but not always in the manner they are presented.

There is sin leading to death (v. 16)—John illustrates praying according to God's will, with the specific example of the "sin leading to death." It is not one particular sin like homosexuality or lying, but whatever premeditated and unconfessed sin is the final one in the tolerance of God. No intercessory prayer will be effective for those who have committed such deliberate high-handed sin. That is, God's discipline with physical death is inevitable in such cases as He seeks to preserve the purity of His church.

Himself (v. 18)—This word is not in the best manuscripts. The better reading in the original language is "keeps him," referring to the fact that God protects the believer.

wicked one (v. 18)—This is a reference to Satan.

does not touch him (v. 18)—The word, used only here and in John 20:17, suggests "to lay hold of" or "to grasp" in order to harm. Because the believer belongs to God, Satan must operate within God's sovereignty and cannot function beyond what God allows, as in the example of Job (Job 2:5; Rom. 16:20).

we are of God (v. 19)—Only two types of people exist in the world according to John: children of God and children of Satan. One belongs either to God or to the evil world system that is Satan's domain. Because the whole world belongs to Satan, Christians should avoid its contamination.

true (v. 20)—The word means "genuine" as opposed to what is false (see v. 21).

God and eternal life (v. 20)—The summation of John's whole letter. The greatest certainty of all, the Incarnation, guarantees the certainty of the rest.

> 20 *And we know that the Son of God has come and has given us an understanding, that we may know Him who is true; and we are in Him who is true, in His Son Jesus Christ. This is the true God and eternal life.*
> 21 *Little children, keep yourselves from idols. Amen.*

keep yourselves from idols (v. 21)—The false beliefs and practices of the false teachers are the idols from which readers are commanded to protect themselves.

1) Summarize John's teaching about prayer.

_____

_____

_____

_____

_____

_____

2) What responsibility do we have for each other, according to verse 16?

_____

_____

_____

_____

_____

3) What did John mean when he talked about the sin leading to death (vv. 16–17; see also the study note)?

_____

_____

_____

_____

4) How did John reiterate his theme of truth in this closing passage (v. 20)?

_____

_____

_____

_____

_____

5) How can a Christian keep himself or herself from idols (v. 21)?

_____

_____

_____

_____

_____

GOING DEEPER

John writes about the certainty we can have that God hears our prayers. For more about prayer, read Hebrews 4:14–16.

14 *Seeing then that we have a great High Priest who has passed through the heavens, Jesus the Son of God, let us hold fast our confession.*
15 *For we do not have a High Priest who cannot sympathize with our weaknesses, but was in all points tempted as we are, yet without sin.*
16 *Let us therefore come boldly to the throne of grace, that we may obtain mercy and find grace to help in time of need.*

EXPLORING THE MEANING

6) What additional light do these verses in Hebrews shed on prayer? Why can we come before God with confidence?

_____

_____

_____

7) How can a believer know if he or she is praying "according to God's will" (1 John 5:14)?

_____

_____

_____

_____

_____

8) According to this passage, why should we regard sin (in ourselves and in others) as a really big deal?

_____

_____

_____

_____

_____

9) Do verses 18–19 promise that Christians will not be attacked by Satan or that we will be exempt from all persecution and testing? How do you know?

_____

_____

_____

_____

Truth for Today

My own experience has taught me much about the different levels of spiritual growth described by the apostle John. When I was a spiritual babe, I was lost in the euphoria of loving the Lord and didn't know much theology. At that time I was easily influenced by anyone's teaching. Later, as I learned the Word of God, false doctrine no longer deceived me; it made me angry. And now, as I have grown in my knowledge of the Word, it's my desire to know God more intimately, which is the final level of growth. Spiritual fathers not only know the Bible, but also know deeply the God who wrote it.

Spiritual growth progresses from knowing you are a Christian to knowing the Word of God to knowing God Himself. The way to know God is to spend your life focusing on His glory, thus learning to understand the fullness of His person. That focus becomes a magnet drawing you upward through the levels of maturity.

REFLECTING ON THE TEXT

10) John said we can know that we have life in Christ. How does knowing this for certain strengthen your faith?

_____

_____

_____

_____

_____

_____

_____

11) As you conclude your study of 1 John, take a moment to quickly skim through the book. Then reflect on the following questions:

⟶ What sin do I need to forsake?

⟶ What new insight do I gain about Christ?

⟶ What promise will I cling to?

⟶ What command do I need to obey?

_____

_____

_____

_____

_____

_____

Personal Response

Write out additional reflections, questions you may have, or a prayer.

Introduction to 2 and 3 John

The epistles are titled "2 John" and "3 John." Second and Third John present the closest approximation in the New Testament to the conventional letter form of the contemporary Greco-Roman world, since they were addressed from an individual to individuals. Second and Third John are the shortest epistles in the New Testament, each containing less than 300 Greek words. Each letter could fit on a single papyrus sheet (see 3 John 13).

Author and Date

The author is the apostle John. He describes himself in both letters as "The Elder" (2 John 1; 3 John 1), which conveys the advanced age of the apostle, his authority, and status during the foundational period of Christianity when he was involved with Jesus' ministry. The precise date of these epistles cannot be determined. Since the wording, subject matter, and circumstances of 2 John closely approximate 1 John (2 John 5 [see 1 John 2:7; 3:11]; v. 6 [see 1 John 5:3]; v. 7 [see 1 John 2:18–26]; v. 9 [see 1 John 2:23]; v. 12 [see 1 John 1:4]), most likely John composed the letter at the same time or soon after 1 John, ca. AD 90–95, during his ministry at Ephesus in the latter part of his life. The book 3 John closely approximates 2 John in structure, style, and vocabulary; hence, John probably composed the third letter at the same time or soon after 2 John.

Background and Setting

The epistle of 2 John deals with the same problem as 1 John. False teachers influenced by the beginnings of Gnostic thought were threatening the church (2 John 7; see 1 John 2:18–19, 22–23; 4:1–3). The strategic difference is that while 1 John has no specific individual or church to whom it was addressed, 2 John has a particular local group or house-church in mind (2 John 1).

The focus of 2 John is that the false teachers were conducting an itinerant ministry among John's congregations, seeking to make converts, and taking advantage of Christian hospitality to advance their cause (2 John 10–11; see Rom. 12:13; Heb. 13:2; 1 Peter 4:9). The individual addressed in the greeting inadvertently or unwisely may have shown these false prophets hospitality, or John may have feared that the false teachers would attempt to take advantage of her kindness (2 John 10–11). The apostle seriously warns his readers against showing hospitality to such deceivers. Although his exhortation may appear on the surface to be harsh or unloving, the acutely dangerous nature of their teaching justified such actions, especially since it threatened to destroy the very foundations of the faith (2 John 9).

The book of 3 John is perhaps the most personal of John's three epistles. While 1 John appears to be a general letter addressed to congregations scattered throughout Asia Minor, and 2 John was sent to a lady and her family (2 John 1), in 3 John the apostle clearly names the sole recipient as "the beloved Gaius" (3 John 1). This makes the epistle one of a few letters in the New Testament addressed strictly to an individual (see Philemon). The name "Gaius" was very common in the first century (Acts 19:29; 20:4; Rom. 16:23; 1 Cor. 1:14), but nothing is known of this individual beyond John's salutation, from which it is implied that he was a member of one of the churches under John's spiritual oversight.

As with 2 John, 3 John focuses on the basic issue of hospitality but from a different perspective. While 2 John warns against showing hospitality to false teachers (2 John 7–11), 3 John condemns the lack of hospitality shown to faithful ministers of the Word (3 John 9–10). Reports came back to the apostle that itinerant teachers known and approved by him (3 John 5–8) had traveled to a certain congregation where they were refused hospitality (lodging and provision) by an individual named Diotrephes, who domineered the assembly (3 John 10). Diotrephes went even further, for he also verbally slandered the apostle John with malicious accusations and excluded anyone from the assembly who dared challenge him.

In contrast, Gaius, a beloved friend of the apostle and faithful adherent to the truth (vv. 1–4), extended the correct standard of Christian hospitality to itinerant ministers. John wrote to commend the type of hospitality exhibited by Gaius to worthy representatives of the gospel (3 John 6–8) and to condemn the high-handed actions of Diotrephes (3 John 10). The apostle promised to correct the situation personally and sent this letter through an individual named Demetrius, whom he commended for his good testimony among the brethren (3 John 10–12).

HISTORICAL AND THEOLOGICAL THEMES

The overall theme of 2 John closely parallels 1 John's theme of a recall to the fundamentals of the faith, or "back to the basics of Christianity" (2 John 4–6). For John, the basics of Christianity are summarized by adherence to truth, love, and obedience.

The apostle, however, conveys an additional but related theme in 2 John: the biblical guidelines for hospitality. Not only are Christians to adhere to the fundamentals of the faith, but the gracious hospitality that is commanded of them (Rom. 12:13) must be discriminating. The basis of hospitality must be common love of or interest in the truth, and Christians must share their love within the confines of that truth. They are not called to universal acceptance of anyone who claims to be a believer. Love must be discerning. Hospitality and kindness must be focused on those who are adhering to the fundamentals of the faith. Otherwise, Christians may actually aid those who are attempting to destroy those basic truths of the faith. Sound doctrine must serve as the test of fellowship and the basis of separation between those who profess to be Christians and those who actually are (2 John 10–11; see Rom. 16:17; Gal. 1:8–9; 2 Thess. 3:6, 14; Tit. 3:10).

The theme of 3 John is the commendation of the proper standards of Christian hospitality and the condemnation for failure to follow those standards.

INTERPRETIVE CHALLENGES

The reference to the "elect lady and her children" (2 John 1) should be understood in a normal, plain sense referring to a particular woman and her children, rather than interpreted in a nonliteral sense as a church and its membership. Similarly, the reference to "the children of your elect sister" (2 John 13) should be understood as a reference to the nieces and/or nephews of the individual addressed in verse 1, rather than metaphorically to a sister church and its membership. In these verses, John conveys greetings to personal acquaintances he has come to know through his ministry.

In 3 John, some think that Diotrephes (3 John 9) may either have been a heretical teacher or at least favored the false teachers who were condemned by 2 John. However, the epistle gives no clear evidence to warrant such a conclusion, especially since one might expect that John would have mentioned Diotrephes's heretical views. The epistle of 3 John indicates that his problems revolved around arrogance and disobedience, which can be problems for the orthodox as well as the heretic.

Additional Notes

10

HOSPITALITY, PART 1

DRAWING NEAR

Define *hospitality*. What similar-sounding words (*hospital*, *host*, etc.) may shed light on the original root meaning of the term?

_____

_____

_____

Who do you know that excels in the ministry of hospitality? Why? What does it look like?

_____

_____

_____

_____

THE CONTEXT

Even a memo from one of the original disciples has great value, particularly if it was inspired by the Holy Spirit. The shortest of the New Testament books, 2 John includes only crucial encouragement and warnings.

The primary difference between 1 John and 2 John has to do with the audience. First John is addressed in a general way to Christians. Second John is written to a particular person—the only New Testament letter specifically addressed to a woman—and a particular church. John's concern in this second epistle seems to have stemmed from this individual's inadvertently or unwisely showing hospitality to false prophets. Although his exhortation to deny hospitality to these itinerant ministers may appear on the surface to be harsh or unloving, the acutely dangerous nature of their deceptive teaching justified such actions, especially since it threatened to destroy the very foundations of the faith.

Similar to John's first letter, the apostle stresses the basic truth of Christ's identity. To deny Christ's humanity is to deny the bodily suffering and sacrifice Christ endured to redeem the world of sin.

KEYS TO THE TEXT

Truth: Five times in the first four verses of 2 John, the apostle uses this term, from the Greek *aletheia*, meaning "corresponding to reality." In the New Testament, *truth* often refers to the facts about God and the accurate teaching of these facts. Here, it refers to the basics or fundamentals of the faith that John has discussed in 1 John (sound belief in Christ, obedience, love) as well as the truths expressed in 2 John (e.g., vv. 4–6). Truth is the necessary condition of unity and, as a result, the basis of hospitality.

UNLEASHING THE TEXT

Read 2 John 1–13, noting the key words and definitions next to the passage.

2 John 1–13 (NKJV)

The Elder (v. 1)—refers to John's advanced age, his spiritual authority over the congregations in Asia Minor, and the strength of his own personal eyewitness testimony to the life of Jesus and all that He taught (vv. 4–6).

the elect lady and her children (v. 1)—Some think that this phrase refers metaphorically to a particular local church, while "her children" would refer to members of the congregation. The more natural understanding in context, however, is that it refers to a particular woman and her children (i.e., offspring) who were well-known to John.

truth . . . abides in us . . . will be with us forever (v. 2)—This is the cognitive truth of God's Word (see Col. 3:16).

1 *The Elder, to the elect lady and her children, whom I love in truth, and not only I, but also all those who have known the truth,*

2 *because of the truth which abides in us and will be with us forever:*

3 *Grace, mercy, and peace will be with you from God the Father and from the Lord Jesus Christ, the Son of the Father, in truth and love.*

4 *I rejoiced greatly that I have found some of your children walking in truth, as we received commandment from the Father.*

5 *And now I plead with you, lady, not as though I wrote a new commandment to you, but that which we have had from the beginning: that we love one another.*

children walking in truth, as we received commandment (v. 4)—The word "walking" has reference to continual walking in the truth, i.e., making obedience to the truth a habit in one's life.

new commandment . . . that we love one another (v. 5)—The word *love* has reference to practicing love as a habit in one's life. Both walking in the truth and in love is the behavior of hospitality.

6 *This is love, that we walk according to His commandments. This is the commandment, that as you have heard from the beginning, you should walk in it.*

7 *For many deceivers have gone out into the world who do not confess Jesus Christ as coming in the flesh. This is a deceiver and an antichrist.*

8 *Look to yourselves, that we do not lose those things we worked for, but that we may receive a full reward.*

9 *Whoever transgresses and does not abide in the doctrine of Christ does not have God. He who abides in the doctrine of Christ has both the Father and the Son.*

10 *If anyone comes to you and does not bring this doctrine, do not receive him into your house nor greet him;*

11 *for he who greets him shares in his evil deeds.*

12 *Having many things to write to you, I did not wish to do so with paper and ink; but I hope to come to you and speak face to face, that our joy may be full.*

13 *The children of your elect sister greet you. Amen.*

This is love, that we walk according to His commandments (v. 6)—John defines love, not as a sentiment or an emotion, but as obedience to God's commands.

many deceivers (v. 7)—John gives limits for Christian hospitality. This is the centerpiece of John's thought in this epistle and expands the first two points.

who do not confess Jesus Christ as coming in the flesh (v. 7)—The original language conveys the idea of a habitual denial of the undiminished deity and humanity of Christ. A biblical Christology maintains that Jesus Christ's nature was both fully God and fully man with all the implications for the fulfillment of redemptive purposes.

do not lose those things we worked for (v. 8)—Although a reward is generally promised Christians for hospitality (Matt. 10:41; 25:40), the idea here is of the fullness of a believer's reward for all the good he has done (see 1 Cor. 3:10–17).

does not abide in the doctrine of Christ does not have God (v. 9)—Failure to be faithful to the fundamental, sound doctrines of the faith (a proper view of the Person and work of Christ, love, obedience) marks a person as having never been born again (1 John 2:23; 3:6–10; 4:20–21; 5:1–3). The word "abide" has the idea of constant adherence and warns that these fundamentals are not open to change or subject to the latest trends or philosophical fads.

do not receive him into your house nor greet him (v. 10)—John's prohibition is not a case of entertaining people who disagree on minor matters; these false teachers were carrying on a regular campaign to destroy the basic, fundamental truths of Christianity.

shares in his evil deeds (v. 11)—Hospitality to such leaders aids the spread of their heresy and leaves the impression of sanctioning the teachings of these antichrists (see 1 John 2:22).

paper and ink (v. 12)—The word "paper" refers to a papyrus sheet. One papyrus sheet could contain the whole letter of 2 John. The term "ink" means "black" and refers to a mixture of water, charcoal, and gum resin that was used to write.

face to face (v. 12)—John literally wrote "mouth to mouth." See Numbers 12:8 in which God spoke to Moses "mouth to mouth."

that our joy may be full (v. 12)—The blessing of hospitality that is rooted in the biblical standards for fellowship is full joy (vv. 12–13) among believers because the truths of the Word are maintained.

The children of your elect sister (v. 13)—John refers to the nieces and/or nephews of the woman ("elect lady") addressed in verse 1, who sent their greetings via John.

1) What is the implied reason that John wrote this letter?

_____

_____

_____

_____

_____

2) What do you learn about the "elect lady"?

_____

_____

_____

_____

_____

3) How did John emphasize the importance of truth?

_____

_____

_____

_____

_____

4) What positive counsel about Christian relationships does John offer?

_____

_____

_____

_____

_____

5) In verse 8, what sobering warning did John give to those who offer indiscriminate fellowship and hospitality to false teachers?

_____

_____

_____

_____

_____

_____

_____

_____

_____

_____

GOING DEEPER

Fighting against false teachers was one of John's main concerns, and it was also a concern of the apostle Paul. Read 1 Timothy 4:1–4 and 2 Corinthians 11:13–15.

1 Tim. 4:1 *Now the Spirit expressly says that in latter times some will depart from the faith, giving heed to deceiving spirits and doctrines of demons,*

2 *speaking lies in hypocrisy, having their own conscience seared with a hot iron,*

3 *forbidding to marry, and commanding to abstain from foods which God created to be received with thanksgiving by those who believe and know the truth.*

4 *For every creature of God is good, and nothing is to be refused if it is received with thanksgiving;*

2 Cor. 11:13 *For such are false apostles, deceitful workers, transforming themselves into apostles of Christ.*

14 *And no wonder! For Satan himself transforms himself into an angel of light.*

15 *Therefore it is no great thing if his ministers also transform themselves into ministers of righteousness, whose end will be according to their works.*

Exploring the Meaning

6) According to these passages, why do believers need to have an intimate acquaintance with the truth?

_____

_____

_____

_____

7) In what way are truth and love related to walking in Christian unity (vv. 4–6)?

_____

_____

_____

_____

8) Why was John so adamant in his epistles that we "confess Jesus Christ as coming in the flesh" (v. 7)?

_____

_____

_____

_____

9) How should Christians respond when people from religious cults (Mormons, Jehovah's Witnesses, Hare Krishnas, and others) knock on the door (v. 10)?

_____

_____

_____

_____

TRUTH FOR TODAY

Upholding the revealed truth of God's Word will inevitably lead to conflict, because many oppose the truth. But if you and I live in the light of eternity, that won't be an obstacle. Any effort we exert in this short life for Christ's sake will be recompensed immeasurably in eternity. That's one reason Paul called it "the *good* warfare" (1 Tim. 1:18 NKJV, emphasis added). J. C. Ryle comments further: "Let us settle it in our minds that the Christian fight is a good fight—really good, truly good, emphatically good. We see only part of it yet. We see the struggle, but not the end; we see the campaign, but not the reward; we see the cross, but not the crown. We see a few humble, broken-spirited, penitent, praying people; . . . but we see not the face of God smiling on them, the kingdom of glory prepared for them . . . There are more good things about the Christian warfare than we see" (*Holiness* [Hertfordshire, England: Evangelical Press, 1989], 62).

REFLECTING ON THE TEXT

10) Are you fighting the good fight? Are you contending for the faith? Is it your desire to obey and proclaim the truth, no matter what the cost? Why or why not?

_____

_____

_____

_____

_____

_____

11) What is the main lesson you are taking away from 2 John?

_____

_____

_____

_____

_____

12) In what specific way do you want to "imitate" the apostle John?

_____

_____

_____

_____

_____

_____

Personal Response

Write out additional reflections, questions you may have, or a prayer.

_____

_____

_____

_____

_____

_____

_____

_____

_____

_____

_____

_____

_____

_____

_____

_____

11

HOSPITALITY, PART 2

DRAWING NEAR

Have you ever had missionaries or someone in the ministry stay with you or your family? What was memorable about showing them hospitality?

_____

_____

_____

_____

_____

Have you ever been involved in a church that was marked by factions or that was dominated by an individual or group? If so, what did you learn from that experience?

_____

_____

_____

_____

THE CONTEXT

Third John is brief and records John's tribute to the practice of hospitality. A simple note to challenge and encourage a leader named Gaius, this epistle uses the behavior of two other leaders as negative and positive examples of effective spiritual leadership. John hoped to expand on this teaching during an upcoming visit to Gaius.

In this most personal of John's three epistles, the apostle commends Gaius for the hospitality and support he had shown to some traveling teachers of the truth. John gives several grounds for practicing hospitality in a "manner worthy of God" (v. 6). Meanwhile, he speaks against Diotrephes, who had refused to extend a welcome to visiting teachers.

KEYS TO THE TEXT

Hospitality: This means to be "hospitable," taken from the Greek word that means "love of strangers." This kind of love is intensely practical, not just emotional. In John's day, hospitality included opening one's home and caring for other needy Christians, such as traveling preachers. It also included opening one's home for church services. John gave some guidelines: one must show hospitality to those who have pure motives (2 John 10). Second, one must show hospitality to those who are not in ministry for money (3 John 7). Third, those who show hospitality participate in the ministries of those to whom hospitality is shown (3 John 8). Fourth, those demonstrating hospitality to genuine teachers share in the deeds (good or bad) of those receiving it (2 John 11).

Church: This word (Greek, *ekklesia*) means literally "an assembly." In secular Greek literature, this term described any gathering of people to an important event or assembly. The writers of the New Testament use this term to mean a local assembly of believers or the worldwide body of believers. John uses *ekklesia* in two ways: "The church" in verse 6 refers to the general group of believers, whereas "the church" in verses 9 and 10 has to be a specific local church. In biblical times, Christians of each city were organized under one group of elders (see Acts 14:23; 15:2, 4; 20:17–18; Titus 1:5). Several "assemblies" of believers, held in various homes, constituted the local church in each city.

UNLEASHING THE TEXT

Read 3 John 1–12, noting the key words and definitions next to the passage.

The Elder (v. 1)—the same term he used for himself in 2 John 1, probably a reference to his age, his apostolic eyewitness status of Jesus' life and also to his official position of authority in the church

Gaius (v. 1)—One of many common names from which Roman parents usually chose a name for one of their sons. Nothing is known of Gaius beyond the mention of his name in the salutation.

whom I love in truth (v. 1)—love that is consistent with the fundamental truths of the faith (see v. 4; 1 John 2:21; 3:19)

I pray (v. 2)—Gaius's spiritual state was so excellent that John prayed that his physical health would match his spiritual vigor

3 John 1–12 (NKJV)

1 *The Elder, to the beloved Gaius, whom I love in truth:*

2 *Beloved, I pray that you may prosper in all things and be in health, just as your soul prospers.*

3 *For I rejoiced greatly when brethren came and testified of the truth that is in you, just as you walk in the truth.*

4 *I have no greater joy than to hear that my children walk in truth.*

5 *Beloved, you do faithfully whatever you do for the brethren and for strangers,*

6 *who have borne witness of your love before the church. If you send them forward on their journey in a manner worthy of God, you will do well,*

7 *because they went forth for His name's sake, taking nothing from the Gentiles.*

8 *We therefore ought to receive such, that we may become fellow workers for the truth.*

9 *I wrote to the church, but Diotrephes, who loves to have the preeminence among them, does not receive us.*

10 *Therefore, if I come, I will call to mind his deeds which he does, prating against us with malicious words. And not content with that, he himself does not receive the brethren, and forbids those who wish to, putting them out of the church.*

when brethren came and testified (v. 3)—Christians continually praised Gaius's exemplary obedience to the fundamentals of the faith. His spiritual reputation was well-known.

you walk in the truth (v. 3)—Gaius's walk matched his talk. His reputation for practicing what he preached was exemplary (2 John 4).

my children (v. 4)—The word "my" is emphatic in the original. John's heart delighted in the proper conduct of his spiritual children in the faith. Those who walk (conduct) in the truth (belief) have integrity. There is no dichotomy between professing and living. He had strong fatherly affection for them (see 1 Cor. 4:14–16; 1 Thess. 2:11; 3:1–10).

you do faithfully (v. 5)—Genuine faith always produces genuine good works (James 2:14–17).

brethren and for strangers (v. 5)—Gaius practiced hospitality not only toward those whom he knew but also to those whom he did not know, especially itinerant gospel preachers that Gaius aided on their journeys.

in a manner worthy of God (v. 6)—The phrase has the connotation of treating people as God would treat them (see Matt. 10:40) and becomes the key manner in which hospitality should be practiced (Matt. 25:40–45).

I wrote to the church (v. 9)—John apparently had written a previous letter to the church, perhaps on the subject of hospitality, but it was lost. Perhaps Diotrephes never read it to the church because he rejected John's authority (see vv. 9–10).

Diotrephes, who loves to have the preeminence (v. 9)—The word "preeminence" has the idea of "desiring to be first." It conveys the idea of someone who is selfish, self-centered, and self-seeking. The language suggests a self-promoting demagogue, who served no one, but wanted all to serve only him.

does not receive us (v. 9)—Diotrephes modeled the opposite of kindness and hospitality to God's servants, even denying John's apostolic authority over the local congregation, and as a result, denying the revelation of God that came through that authority. His pride endeavored to supplant the rule of Christ through John in the church. Diotrephes's character was the very opposite of the gentle and loving Gaius who readily showed hospitality.

if I come, I will call to mind his deeds (v. 10)—John's apostolic authority meant that Diotrephes had to answer for his behavior. The apostle did not overlook this usurping of Christ's place in the church.

does not receive the brethren (v. 10)—Accepting John's authority (v. 9), as well as being hospitable to the traveling ministers, would directly threaten the authority that Diotrephes coveted.

He who does good is of God, but he who does evil has not seen God (v. 11)—John's statement indicates that Diotrephes's actions proved that he was never a Christian.

Demetrius (v. 12)—As with Gaius, Demetrius was a very common name in the Roman world (Acts 19:24, 38). Nothing is known of him apart from this epistle. He may have delivered this letter, which also would serve to commend him to Gaius.

from the truth itself (v. 12)—Demetrius was an excellent role model preeminently because he practiced the truth of God's Word in his life.

11 *Beloved, do not imitate what is evil, but what is good. He who does good is of God, but he who does evil has not seen God.*

12 *Demetrius has a good testimony from all, and from the truth itself. And we also bear witness, and you know that our testimony is true.*

1) For what actions and traits was Gaius commended?

_____

_____

_____

_____

_____

2) What did John say in this epistle about "missionaries"?

_____

_____

_____

_____

_____

3) What four things was Diotrephes guilty of (see v. 10)?

_____

_____

_____

_____

_____

4) For what actions and traits was Demetrius complimented?

_____

_____

_____

_____

_____

5) What guidelines or principles concerning Christian hospitality are found in 3 John?

_____

_____

_____

_____

_____

_____

Going Deeper

John exposed Diotrephes's pride and hard heart. For more about how we are to minister with humility, read Philippians 2:5–11.

5   *Let this mind be in you which was also in Christ Jesus,*
6   *who, being in the form of God, did not consider it robbery to be equal with God,*
7   *but made Himself of no reputation, taking the form of a bondservant, and coming in the likeness of men.*
8   *And being found in appearance as a man, He humbled Himself and became obedient to the point of death, even the death of the cross.*
9   *Therefore God also has highly exalted Him and given Him the name which is above every name,*
10 *that at the name of Jesus every knee should bow, of those in heaven, and of those on earth, and of those under the earth,*
11 *and that every tongue should confess that Jesus Christ is Lord, to the glory of God the Father.*

Exploring the Meaning

6) What is the difference between Christ's behavior and attitudes described in Philippians and Diotrephes's behavior and attitudes?

_____

_____

_____

_____

_____

_____

7) Why is sharing Christian hospitality with others important?

_____

_____

_____

_____

_____

8) John rejoiced that his "children" walked in the truth (vv. 3–4). What "truth" was he referring to?

_____

_____

_____

_____

_____

9) What are the high points and low points of John's third letter?

_____

_____

_____

_____

_____

Truth for Today

True followers of Christ should not only meet the needs of believers and unbelievers whom they encounter, but they should also look for opportunities to help those they don't know. This is the scriptural definition of hospitality. Hebrews 13:2 instructs us, "Do not forget to entertain strangers, for by so doing some have unwittingly entertained angels" (NKJV). You should view any opportunity to demonstrate hospitality as a happy privilege, not a drudging duty. Gaius undoubtedly had that sort of righteous attitude in his hospitality toward itinerant teachers, because the apostle John commended him: "Beloved, you do faithfully whatever you do for the brethren and for strangers, who have borne witness of your love before the church" (3 John 5 NKJV).

Reflecting on the Text

10) What has been your most memorable experience of giving or receiving Christian hospitality?

_____

_____

_____

_____

11) What traits of Gaius or Demetrius do you want to emulate?

_____

_____

_____

_____

12) List four concrete things you and your family will do in the future to be more hospitable to a full-time vocational missionary or minister.

_____

_____

_____

_____

Personal Response

Write out additional reflections, questions you may have, or a prayer.

_____

_____

_____

_____

_____

_____

_____

_____

_____

_____

_____

_____

_____

_____

_____

_____

_____

_____

_____

_____

_____

_____

_____

_____

_____

_____

_____

_____

Introduction to Jude

Jude, which is rendered "Judah" in Hebrew and "Judas" in Greek, was named after its author (v. 1), one of the four half-brothers of Christ (Matt. 13:55; Mark 6:3). As the fourth shortest New Testament book (Philemon, 2 John, and 3 John are shorter), Jude is the last of eight general epistles. Jude does not quote the Old Testament directly, but there are at least nine allusions to it. Contextually, this "epistolary sermon" could be called "The Acts of the Apostates."

AUTHOR AND DATE

Although Jude (Judas) was a common name in Palestine (at least eight Judes are named in the New Testament), the author of this epistle generally has been accepted as Jude, Christ's half-brother. He is not the same person as the apostle Judas, the son of James (Luke 6:16; Acts 1:13). Several lines of thought lead to this conclusion: (1) Jude's appeal to being the "brother of James," the leader of the Jerusalem Council (Acts 15) and another half-brother of Jesus (v. 1; see Gal. 1:19); (2) Jude's salutation being similar to James (see James 1:1); and (3) Jude's refraining from identifying himself as an apostle (v. 1), but rather distinguishing between himself and the apostles (v. 17).

The doctrinal and moral apostasy discussed by Jude (vv. 4–18) closely parallels that of 2 Peter (2:1–3:4), and it is believed that Peter's writing predated Jude for several reasons: (1) Second Peter anticipates the coming of false teachers (2 Pet. 2:1–2; 3:3), whereas Jude deals with their arrival (vv. 4, 11–12, 17–18); and (2) Jude quotes directly from 2 Peter 3:3 and acknowledges that it is from an apostle (vv. 17–18). Since no mention of Jerusalem's destruction in AD 70 was made by Jude, it was almost certainly written before the destruction of Jerusalem (ca. AD 68–70). Although Jude did travel on missionary trips with other brothers and their wives (1 Cor. 9:5), it is most likely that he wrote from Jerusalem.

Although Jude earlier had rejected Jesus as Messiah (John 7:1–9), he, along with other half-brothers of our Lord, was converted after Christ's resurrection (Acts 1:14). Because of his relation to Jesus, his eyewitness knowledge of the resurrected Christ, and the content of this epistle, it was acknowledged as inspired and was included in the Muratorian Canon (AD 170). The early questions about its canonicity also tend to support that it was written after 2 Peter. If Peter had quoted Jude, there would have been no question about canonicity, since Peter would thereby have given Jude apostolic affirmation. Clement of Rome (ca. AD 96) plus Clement of Alexandria (ca. AD 200) also alluded to the authenticity of Jude. Its diminutive size and Jude's quotations from uninspired writings account for any misplaced questions about its canonicity.

BACKGROUND AND SETTING

Jude lived at a time when Christianity was under severe political attack from Rome and aggressive spiritual infiltration from Gnostic-like apostates and libertines who sowed abundant seed for a gigantic harvest of doctrinal error. It could be that this was the forerunner to full-blown Gnosticism, which the apostle John would confront more than twenty-five years later in his epistles. Except for John, who lived at the close of the century, all of the other apostles had been martyred, and Christianity was thought to be extremely vulnerable. Thus, Jude called the church to fight for the truth in the midst of intense spiritual warfare.

HISTORICAL AND THEOLOGICAL THEMES

Jude is the only New Testament book devoted exclusively to confronting "apostasy," meaning defection from the true, biblical faith (vv. 3, 17). Apostates are described elsewhere in 2 Thessalonians 2:10; Hebrews 10:29; 2 Peter 2:1–22; and 1 John 2:18–23. He wrote to condemn the apostates and to urge believers to contend for the faith. He called for discernment on the part of the church and a rigorous defense of biblical truth. He followed the earlier examples of: Christ (Matt. 7:15ff.; 16:6–12; 24:11ff; Rev. 2, 3); Paul (Acts 20:29–30; 1 Tim. 4:1; 2 Tim. 3:1–5; 4:3–4); Peter (2 Pet. 2:1–2; 3:34); and John (1 John 4:1–6; 2 John 6–11).

Jude is replete with historical illustrations from the Old Testament, which include: the Exodus (v. 5), Satan's rebellion (v. 6), Sodom and Gomorrah (v. 7), Moses' death (v. 9), Cain (v. 11), Balaam (v. 11), Korah (v. 11), Enoch (vv. 14–15), and Adam (v. 14).

Jude vividly described the apostates in terms of their character and unconscionable activities (vv. 4, 8, 10, 16, 18, 19). Additionally, he borrowed from nature to illustrate the futility of their teaching (vv. 12–13). While Jude never commented on the specific content of their false teaching, it was enough to demonstrate that their degenerate personal lives and fruitless ministries betrayed their attempts to teach error as though it were truth. This emphasis on character repeats the constant theme regarding false teachers—their personal corruption. While their teaching is clever, subtle, deceptive, enticing, and delivered in various forms, the easiest way to recognize false teachers is to look behind their false spiritual fronts and discern their wicked lives (2 Pet. 2:10, 12, 18–19).

INTERPRETIVE CHALLENGES

Because there are no doctrinal issues discussed, the challenges of this letter have to do with judging the correct interpretation of the text. Jude does quote from noncanonical, pseudepigraphal sources (in which the actual author was not the one named in its title), such as *1 Enoch* (v. 14) and the *Assumption of Moses* (v. 9) to support his points. Was this acceptable? Since Jude was writing under the inspiration of the Holy Spirit (2 Tim. 3:16; 2 Pet. 1:20–21) and included material that was accurate and true in its affirmations, he did no differently from Paul (see Acts 17:28; 1 Cor. 15:33; Titus 1:12).

NOTES

~ 12 ~
APOSTASY

Jude

DRAWING NEAR

Which of the following potentially destructive cultural trends do you see infiltrating the Western church? Or influencing your own local church?

- A rise in shallow spirituality and self-help gurus, with a decline in solid biblical teaching

- The growing fixation with fashion, fitness, thinness to the detriment of personal character and spiritual growth

- Widespread attempts at "marketing" the church, running local congregations like businesses

- Rampant immorality and hedonism (including the proliferation of adultery and pornography)

- Culture's shockingly low view of marriage, the skyrocketing rates of cohabitation, and divorce

- Unbridled materialism and consumerism

- The postmodern "all things are OK" mind-set

- Efforts to make the gospel "seeker-friendly," man-centered, and non-offensive

Why are these trends and attitudes so dangerous to Christians?

_____

_____

_____

_____

_____

_____

THE CONTEXT

Jude was the second half-brother of Jesus to write a New Testament letter. Like his brother James, Jude became a significant leader in the church in Jerusalem.

The exact audience of believers with whom Jude corresponded is unknown but seems to be Jewish in light of Jude's illustrations. He undoubtedly wrote to a region recently plagued by false teachers.

Jude opens his attack on apostasy by first addressing believers. He concludes his epistle by bolstering the courage of believers in Christ's power. Jude proclaims Jesus as the one "who is able to keep you from stumbling, and to present you faultless" (v. 24 NKJV). Thus, Jude called the church to fight—in the midst of intense spiritual warfare—for the truth. Jude presents a great warning shout on behalf of his brother the Lord to stand firm!

Keys to the Text

Apostasy: From the Greek word *apostasia*, meaning "falling away." Apostates were false teachers pretending to be true, who on the surface looked like the real thing, but whose intentions were to lead God's people astray. They were Satan's counterfeits, most likely posing as itinerant teachers. Their stealth made them dangerous. They were characterized by three features: they were ungodly, they perverted grace, and they denied Christ.

Keep You: The word translated "keep" in Jude 24 (Greek *phylasso*) means "guard or watch," and was used in ancient times of keeping valuables in a safe place. It was also a military term that described a soldier on watch, who was accountable with his own life to protect what was entrusted to his care. It conveys the basic idea of securing in the midst of an attack. Jude uses it to remind us that no matter what our spiritual enemies may throw against us, the power of Christ will sustain the sincere believer from falling to the temptation of apostasy.

Unleashing the Text

Read Jude 1–25, noting the key words and definitions next to the passage.

called (v. 1)—This refers not to a general invitation to salvation, but to God's irresistible, elective call to salvation.

God the Father (v. 1)—The plan of salvation and its fulfillment come from God, who is not only Father in the sense of creation and origin of all that exists, but is also "God our Savior" (v. 25).

preserved (v. 1)—God not only initiates salvation, but He also completes it through Christ, thus preserving or keeping the believer secure for eternal life (see John 6:37–44; 10:28–30; Rom. 8:31–39; 1 Pet. 1:3–5).

Jude 1–25 (NKJV)

1 *Jude, a bondservant of Jesus Christ, and brother of James, to those who are called, sanctified by God the Father, and preserved in Jesus Christ:*

2 *Mercy, peace, and love be multiplied to you.*

3 Beloved, while I was very diligent to write to you concerning our common salvation, I found it necessary to write to you exhorting you to contend earnestly for the faith which was once for all delivered to the saints.

4 For certain men have crept in unnoticed, who long ago were marked out for this condemnation, ungodly men, who turn the grace of our God into lewdness and deny the only Lord God and our Lord Jesus Christ.

5 But I want to remind you, though you once knew this, that the Lord, having saved the people out of the land of Egypt, afterward destroyed those who did not believe.

6 And the angels who did not keep their proper domain, but left their own abode, He has reserved in everlasting chains under darkness for the judgment of the great day;

7 as Sodom and Gomorrah, and the cities around them in a similar manner to these, having given themselves over to sexual immorality and gone after strange flesh, are set forth as an example, suffering the vengeance of eternal fire.

I found it necessary (v. 3)—Jude had intended to write a letter on salvation as the common blessing enjoyed by all believers, but he was compelled, instead, to write a call to battle for the truth in light of the arrival of apostate teachers.

contend earnestly (v. 3)—Jude wrote this urgent imperative for Christians to wage war against error in all forms and fight strenuously for the truth, like a soldier who has been entrusted with a sacred task of guarding a holy treasure (see 1 Tim. 6:12; 2 Tim. 4:7).

once for all delivered . . . saints (v. 3)—God's revelation was delivered once as a unit, at the completion of the Scripture, and is not to be edited by either deletion or addition (see Deut. 4:2; 12:32; Rev. 22:18–19).

certain men . . . crept in unnoticed (v. 4)—These were infiltrating, false teachers pretending to be true, who on the surface looked like the real thing, but whose intentions were to lead God's people astray.

long ago . . . marked out (v. 4)—Apostasy and apostates in general were written about and condemned many centuries before, such as illustrated in verses 5–7 and spoken of as Enoch did in verses 14–16.

ungodly men (v. 4)—Literally "impious" or "without worship." Their lack of reverence for God was demonstrated by their infiltration of the church of God to corrupt it and gain riches from its people.

saved . . . destroyed (v. 5)—God miraculously delivered the people of Israel out of Egyptian bondage (Ex. 12:51; Deut. 4:34) only to have them respond in unbelief, doubting that He could bring them into the Promised Land (Num. 13:25–14:4).

angels . . . did not keep (v. 6)—This apostasy of fallen angels is described in Gen. 6:1–3 as an evil that possessed men, who then cohabited with women.

sexual immorality . . . strange flesh (v. 7)—This refers to both the heterosexual (Gen. 19:8) and homosexual lusts (Gen. 19:4–5) of the residents. See Leviticus 18:22; 20:13; Romans 1:27; 1 Corinthians 6:9; and 1 Timothy 1:10 for the absolute condemnation of homosexual activity.

eternal fire (v. 7)—The destruction of Sodom and Gomorrah illustrates God's fire of earthly judgment (see Rev. 16:8–9; 20:9), which was only a preview of the fire in eternal hell that can never be quenched (see Matt. 3:12; 18:8; 25:41; Mark 9:43–44, 46, 48; Luke 3:17; Rev. 19:20; 20:14–15; 21:8).

these dreamers (v. 8)—This refers to a confused state of the soul or abnormal imagination, producing delusions and sensual confusion. These men's minds were numb to the truth of God's Word so that, being beguiled and deluded, they fantasized wicked perversions, being blind and deaf to reality and truth.

Michael . . . archangel (v. 9)—the chief angel of God who especially watches over Israel (Dan. 10:13, 21; 12:1) and leads the holy angels (Rev. 12:7)

body of Moses (v. 9)—Moses died on Mount Nebo in Moab without having entered the Promised Land and was secretly buried in a place not known to man (Deut. 34:5–6). It would likely be that this confrontation took place as Michael buried Moses to prevent Satan from using Moses' body for some diabolical purpose not stated.

8 *Likewise also these dreamers defile the flesh, reject authority, and speak evil of dignitaries.*

9 *Yet Michael the archangel, in contending with the devil, when he disputed about the body of Moses, dared not bring against him a reviling accusation, but said, "The Lord rebuke you!"*

10 *But these speak evil of whatever they do not know; and whatever they know naturally, like brute beasts, in these things they corrupt themselves.*

11 *Woe to them! For they have gone in the way of Cain, have run greedily in the error of Balaam for profit, and perished in the rebellion of Korah.*

12 *These are spots in your love feasts, while they feast with you without fear, serving only themselves. They are clouds without water, carried about by the winds; late autumn trees without fruit, twice dead, pulled up by the roots;*

reviling accusation (v. 9)—Rather than personally cursing such a powerful angel as Satan, Michael deferred to the ultimate, sovereign power of God, following the example of the Angel of the Lord in Zechariah 3:2. This is the supreme illustration of how Christians are to deal with Satan and demons. Believers are not to address them, but rather to seek the Lord's intervening power against them.

whatever . . . whatever (v. 10)—Apostates are intellectually arrogant and spiritually ignorant because they are blinded by Satan (2 Cor. 4:4), and spiritual matters are beyond their unregenerate capacity to understand (1 Cor. 2:14).

error of Balaam (v. 11)—See Numbers 22–25. For a large financial reward, Balaam devised a plan for Balak, king of Moab, to entice Israel into a compromising situation with idolatry and immorality, which would bring God's own judgment on His people (see Num. 31:16; Rev. 2:14).

rebellion of Korah (v. 11)—Korah, plus 250 Jewish leaders, rejected the God-appointed leadership of Moses and Aaron in an attempt to impose his will upon God and the people (see Num. 16); as a result, they were all judged by God.

spots (v. 12)—"Spots" can be taken as "hidden rocks" or "reefs" or as "stains." These apostates were dirt spots, filth on the garment of the church. Or more likely, what God intended for the church as smooth sailing, they turned into a potential shipwreck through their presence.

love feasts (v. 12)—"Love feasts" were the regular gatherings of the early church to partake of the bread and cup, plus share a common meal (see 1 Cor. 11:20–30).

clouds without water (v. 12)—Apostates promise spiritual life but are like empty clouds that bring the hope of rain, but actually deliver nothing but dryness and death (see Prov. 25:14). They preach a false gospel that leads only to hell.

trees without fruit (v. 12)—Apostates promise a spiritual feast, but instead deliver famine (see Luke 16:6–9).

13 *raging waves of the sea, foaming up their own shame; wandering stars for whom is reserved the blackness of darkness forever.*

14 *Now Enoch, the seventh from Adam, prophesied about these men also, saying, "Behold, the Lord comes with ten thousands of His saints,*

15 *to execute judgment on all, to convict all who are ungodly among them of all their ungodly deeds which they have committed in an ungodly way, and of all the harsh things which ungodly sinners have spoken against Him."*

16 *These are grumblers, complainers, walking according to their own lusts; and they mouth great swelling words, flattering people to gain advantage.*

17 *But you, beloved, remember the words which were spoken before by the apostles of our Lord Jesus Christ:*

18 *how they told you that there would be mockers in the last time who would walk according to their own ungodly lusts.*

19 *These are sensual persons, who cause divisions, not having the Spirit.*

20 *But you, beloved, building yourselves up on your most holy faith, praying in the Holy Spirit,*

21 *keep yourselves in the love of God, looking for the mercy of our Lord Jesus Christ unto eternal life.*

raging waves (v. 13)—Apostates promise powerful ministry, but are quickly exposed as wreakers of havoc and workers of worthless shame (see Isa. 57:20).

wandering stars (v. 13)—Likely refers to a meteor or shooting star, which has an uncontrolled moment of brilliance and then fades away forever into nothing. Apostates promise enduring spiritual direction, but deliver a brief, aimless, and worthless flash.

Enoch (v. 14)—Following the genealogy of Genesis 5:1–24 and 1 Chronicles 1:1–3, Enoch was the seventh in the line of Adam. Because Enoch "walked with God," he was taken directly to heaven without having to die (see Gen. 5:24; Heb. 11:5).

prophesied about these men (v. 14)—The source of this information was the Holy Spirit who inspired Jude. The fact that it was recorded in the pseudepigraphal and nonbiblical *Book of Enoch* had no effect on its accuracy.

mouth great . . . words (v. 16)—They speak arrogantly, pompously, and even magnificently, but with empty, lifeless words of no spiritual value. Their message has external attractiveness, but is void of the powerful substance of divine truth.

flattering people (v. 16)—They tell people what they want to hear for their own profit (see 2 Tim. 4:3–4), rather than proclaiming the truth of God's Word for the hearers' benefit.

words . . . by the apostles (v. 17)—The apostles had warned the coming generation about apostates, so that they would be prepared and not be taken by surprise.

sensual persons (v. 19)—Apostate teachers advertise themselves as having the highest spiritual knowledge, but are actually attracted to the most debased levels of life. They are "soulish," not "spiritual."

building (v. 20)—True believers have a sure foundation (1 Cor. 3:11) and cornerstone (Eph. 2:20) in Jesus Christ.

praying in the Holy Spirit (v. 20)—not a call to some ecstatic form of prayer, but simply a call to pray consistently in the will and power of the Spirit, as one would pray in the name of Jesus Christ (see Rom. 8:26–27)

keep (v. 21)—This imperative establishes the believer's responsibility to be obedient and faithful by living out his salvation (see Phil. 2:12) while God works out His will (see Phil. 2:13).

compassion (v. 22)—These victims of the apostate teachers need mercy and patience because they have not yet reached a firm conclusion about Christ and eternal life, and so remain doubters who could possibly be swayed to the truth.

with exceeding joy (v. 24)—This refers primarily to the joy of the Savior (see Heb. 12:2) but also includes the joy of believers (see 1 Pet. 1:8). Joy is the dominant expression of heaven.

alone is wise (v. 25)—Divine wisdom is embodied by Christ alone (see 1 Cor. 1:24, 30; Col. 2:3) and not by any human person or group, like the apostates.

22 *And on some have compassion, making a distinction;*

23 *but others save with fear, pulling them out of the fire, hating even the garment defiled by the flesh.*

24 *Now to Him who is able to keep you from stumbling, and to present you faultless before the presence of His glory with exceeding joy,*

25 *To God our Savior, Who alone is wise, be glory and majesty, dominion and power, both now and forever. Amen.*

1) Jude spoke of God's "call." Look at the following New Testament passages and write down what they reveal about the blessings that God's call yields.

1 Corinthians 1:9—

_____

_____

_____

1 Corinthians 7:15—

_____

_____

_____

Galatians 5:13—

_____

_____

_____

Ephesians 4:1, 4—

_____

_____

_____

1 Peter 1:15—

_____

_____

_____

1 Peter 3:9—

_____

_____

_____

1 Peter 5:10—

_____

_____

2) What did Jude mean by "the faith which was once . . . delivered to the saints" (v. 3)?

_____

_____

_____

_____

_____

3) On what figures and events from biblical history did Jude base his warnings?

_____

_____

_____

_____

_____

4) How are the false teachers described?

_____

_____

_____

_____

5) What does the word *apostasy* mean, and how does Jude characterize an apostate?

_____

_____

_____

_____

6) What specific aspects of our relationship with God through Christ are lifted up in the doxology of verses 24–25?

_____

_____

_____

_____

_____

GOING DEEPER

In his second epistle, the apostle Peter wrote at length about the danger of false teachers and apostates. Read 2 Peter 2:1–17.

1   *But there were also false prophets among the people, even as there will be false teachers among you, who will secretly bring in destructive heresies, even denying the Lord who bought them, and bring on themselves swift destruction.*

2   *And many will follow their destructive ways, because of whom the way of truth will be blasphemed.*

3   *By covetousness they will exploit you with deceptive words; for a long time their judgment has not been idle, and their destruction does not slumber.*

4 *For if God did not spare the angels who sinned, but cast them down to hell and delivered them into chains of darkness, to be reserved for judgment;*

5 *and did not spare the ancient world, but saved Noah, one of eight people, a preacher of righteousness, bringing in the flood on the world of the ungodly;*

6 *and turning the cities of Sodom and Gomorrah into ashes, condemned them to destruction, making them an example to those who afterward would live ungodly;*

7 *and delivered righteous Lot, who was oppressed by the filthy conduct of the wicked*

8 *(for that righteous man, dwelling among them, tormented his righteous soul from day to day by seeing and hearing their lawless deeds)—*

9 *then the Lord knows how to deliver the godly out of temptations and to reserve the unjust under punishment for the day of judgment,*

10 *and especially those who walk according to the flesh in the lust of uncleanness and despise authority. They are presumptuous, self-willed. They are not afraid to speak evil of dignitaries,*

11 *whereas angels, who are greater in power and might, do not bring a reviling accusation against them before the Lord.*

12 *But these, like natural brute beasts made to be caught and destroyed, speak evil of the things they do not understand, and will utterly perish in their own corruption,*

13 *and will receive the wages of unrighteousness, as those who count it pleasure to carouse in the daytime. They are spots and blemishes, carousing in their own deceptions while they feast with you,*

14 *having eyes full of adultery and that cannot cease from sin, enticing unstable souls. They have a heart trained in covetous practices, and are accursed children.*

15 *They have forsaken the right way and gone astray, following the way of Balaam the son of Beor, who loved the wages of unrighteousness;*

16 *but he was rebuked for his iniquity: a dumb donkey speaking with a man's voice restrained the madness of the prophet.*

17 *These are wells without water, clouds carried by a tempest, for whom is reserved the blackness of darkness forever.*

Exploring the Meaning

7) How, and with what tone, does Peter describe these false teachers? What will be their end?

_____

_____

_____

_____

_____

_____

8) What ideas did Jude quote and borrow from Peter's epistle?

_____

_____

_____

_____

_____

_____

9) How does one contend for the faith without being belligerent and harsh?

_____

_____

_____

_____

_____

10) What is the antidote Jude gives to falling for false teaching (vv. 20–23)?

_____

_____

_____

_____

TRUTH FOR TODAY

In Jude's brief letter to believers, the apostle firmly warns against false prophets and tells us how to respond to them. "Keep yourselves in the love of God" (Jude 21 NKJV). Our primary response to false teaching is simply to be right with God in the first place, to make sure we are in fellowship with Him and receiving His blessing and power.

Sometimes the battle really gets hot and heavy. That's what motivated Jude to write his letter, which is about apostasy or a departure from the faith. But in the midst of that apostasy and wickedness there was a group of true believers. Not only did they see false teaching and corruption coming into the church, but also all the values of society going down the drain. Undoubtedly they were apprehensive about being swept away by all that wickedness. But Jude wrote that there was no reason to fear, because true believers are "called, sanctified by God the Father, and preserved in Jesus Christ" (v. 1 NKJV). The Greek term used stresses a watchful care to guard something as cherished as a priceless treasure. What was Jude saying? That Christ guards us from all evil.

REFLECTING ON THE TEXT

11) What is one important "take away" truth you've gleaned from Jude's letter? How can you apply that to your life now?

---

12) In what specific ways has your mind-set or behavior changed as a result of your studies in 1, 2, and 3 John and Jude?

Personal Response

Write out additional reflections, questions you may have, or a prayer.

_____

_____

_____

_____

_____

_____

_____

_____

_____

_____

_____

_____

_____

_____

_____

_____

_____

_____

_____

_____

_____

_____

_____

_____

_____

Additional Notes

ADDITIONAL NOTES

ADDITIONAL NOTES

ADDITIONAL NOTES

The MacArthur Bible Study Series

Revised and updated, the MacArthur Study Guide Series continues to be one of the bestselling study guide series on the market today. For small group or individual use, intriguing questions and new material take the participant deeper into God's Word.

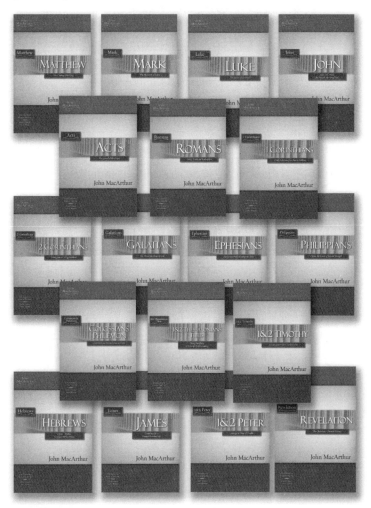

Available at your local Christian Bookstore or www.nelsonimpact.com

NELSON IMPACT
A Division of Thomas Nelson Publishers
Since 1798

www.thomasnelson.com

Look for these exciting titles by John MacArthur

Experiencing the Passion of Christ

Experiencing the Passion of Christ Student Edition

Twelve Extraordinary Women Workbook

Twelve Ordinary Men Workbook

Welcome to the Family:
What to Expect Now That You're a Christian

What the Bible Says About Parenting:
Biblical Principles for Raising Godly Children

Hard to Believe Workbook:
The High Cost and Infinite Value of Following Jesus

The John MacArthur Study Library for PDA

The MacArthur Bible Commentary

The MacArthur Study Bible, NKJV

The MacArthur Topical Bible, NKJV

The MacArthur Bible Commentary

The MacArthur Bible Handbook

The MacArthur Bible Studies series

Available at your local Christian bookstore
or visit www.thomasnelson.com

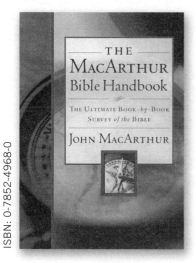
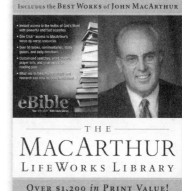

NELSON IMPACT

A Division of Thomas Nelson Publishers

Since 1798

The Nelson Impact Team is here to answer your questions
and suggestions as to how we can create more resources
that benefit you, your family, and your community.

Contact us at Impact@thomasnelson.com